Pet Owner's Guide to the

JACK RUSSELL
TERRIER

JOHN VALENTINE

RINGPRESS

RINGPRESS

Published by Ringpress Books Limited,
PO Box 8, Lydney, Gloucestershire
GL15 6YD, United Kingdom.

First Published 1997
© 1997 Ringpress Books Limited.
All rights reserved

ISBN 1 86054 007 4

Printed and bound in Hong Kong

Contents

Tiverton Buster, owned and bred by John Valentine.

About the author

John Valentine has owned Jack Russell Terriers since childhood, and has acquired a huge amount of knowledge on the breed. He has now bred seven generations of Jack Russells and shown them with great success at Hunt Shows. In 1990 the Parson Jack Russell Terrier received official Kennel Club recognition in the UK, enabling enthusiasts to show their dogs at Championship shows, including the prestigious Crufts show. John has won many awards at Championship shows, and he also judges the breed at Championship level.

Acknowledgements

Thanks to Neil Maxwell Young, Shiela Atter, Cass Samways, and Anne Milne for photographic contributions.

Chapter One

INTRODUCING THE JACK RUSSELL

EARLY HISTORY

Most people will have come across a
small,, white, docked terrier, which is
referred to as a 'Jack Russell Terrier'. As
far back as the end of the eighteenth
century there is pictorial evidence of the
existence of white-bodied, or
predominantly white-bodied, terriers of
the type known today as the Jack Russell
Terrier. Few of today's popular breeds of
dog can be reliably traced back as far as
this in an unchanged state. An engraving
by Scott shows a terrier named Pitch,
published in 1810, which was taken from
an oil painting by Sawrey Gilpin. This
depicts, unmistakably, the type of terrier
that was to be favoured by the Reverend
John Russell, the man who gave the
breed its name in the nineteenth century.
Pitch was born around 1785 and was
owned by Colonel Thornton. He is
shown as being white-bodied with the
characteristic head and tail markings, and
although he may appear a little deep in
the chest for the breed enthusiasts of
today, he is still quite typical of the breed
of terrier which is now recognised as the
Parson Jack Russell Terrier.

THE REVEREND JOHN RUSSELL

John Russell, the founder of the Jack
Russell breed, was born in 1795 in
Dartmouth. His father was, at that time,
Rector of Iddesleigh in North Devon.
He was a keen huntsman, an interest that
his son was swift to develop. Inevitably,

this led to an involvement with the type
of terrier used for bolting foxes. In 1819
John Russell, who was by then a curate,
acquired a terrier from a milkman. The
terrier was known as Trump, and this
dog has gone down in history as the first
Jack Russell Terrier. This was the start of
John Russell's lifelong interest in
developing the perfect sporting
companion, and Trump left a legacy of
game, sporting little terriers, bearing the
Parson's name, that are highly prized to
this day.

An oil painting of Trump, by Mary
Palmer, was painted in the Parson's own
lifetime, and he reputedly regarded it as a
good likeness. This shows Trump as
being white-bodied, with head and tail
markings similar to Colonel Thornton's
Pitch from the previous century. She was
described by John Russell's curate
E.W.L. Davies (who wrote a book called
*The Outdoor Life and Times of John
Russell*), as having a patch of dark tan
over each eye and ear, with a similar dot,
not larger than a penny piece, at the root
of her tail. Her coat was thick, close and
wiry, to protect from the wet and cold,
and her legs were as straight as arrows,
with her whole frame indicative of
hardihood and endurance. Her size and
height are compared to that of a full-
grown vixen fox.

When John Russell died on April 28th
1883, in his 88th year, he had devoted
over 60 years of his life to breeding

foxing terriers like Trump, during which time his reputation as a breeder of terriers, and as a huntsman, had become widespread. The Reverend John Russell was buried at Swymbridge, in Devon, where his funeral was attended by at least a thousand people. The Parson was not only a respected breeder of terriers – he was also well-liked and respected by his parishioners.

THE TERRIER'S WORK
The name terrier is generally accepted as being derived from the Latin 'terra' meaning earth. The Jack Russell Terrier was bred to go to ground, i.e. to work in the earth, for the purpose of bolting foxes. John Russell required that his terriers were not only of the conformation to enable them to go to ground after the fox, but also that they possessed the stamina and build to be able to keep up with the hounds.

It is interesting to quote a story from E.W.L. Davies, as told to him by John Russell himself, concerning the activities of one of his terriers, known as Tip. The story concerns a particular fox which had made its escape from the hounds by seeking refuge in the "fathomless earths of Gray's Holt", so-called after "Gray", the old Devonshire name for badger, many of which had occupied the spot.

"Again, we found that fox a second time; and now to my infinite surprise I saw Tip going off at full speed in quite a different direction.

" 'He's off, sir, to Gray's Holt; I know he is,' shouted Jack Yelland, the whip, as he called my attention to the line of country the dog was taking.

"That proved to be the case. The fox had scarcely been ten minutes on foot when the dog either by instinct, or, as I believe, by some power akin to reason putting two and two together, came to the conclusion that the real object of the fox was to gain Gray's Holt, although the hounds were by no means pointing in that direction. It was exactly as if the dog had said to himself: 'No, no! You're the same fox, I know, that gave us the slip once before; but you're not going to play us that trick again.'

"Tip's deduction was accurately correct; for the fox, after a turn or two in cover, put his nose directly for Gray's Holt; hoping, beyond a doubt, to gain that city of refuge once more, and then to whisk his brush in the face of his foes. But in this manoeuvre he was fairly out-generalled by the dog's tactics. Tip had taken the short cut - the cord of the arc - and, as the hounds raced by at some distance off, there I saw him," continued Russell, "dancing about on Gray's Holt, throwing his tongue frantically, and doing his utmost, by noise and gesture, to scare away the fox from approaching the earths.

"Perfect success crowned the manoeuvre: the fox, not daring to face the lion in his path, gave the spot a wide berth."

Perhaps this account sums up as well as anything exactly what John Russell required of terriers.

THE HERITAGE
Carlisle Tack, born in 1884, and therefore only one year after Parson Russell's death, is portrayed in a drawing by Arthur Wardle. Tack's pedigree shows that he was descended from some of John Russell's own terriers and, although lacking in the head and tail markings of Trump, he shows a definite similarity to that first terrier acquired some 65 years before. Fashions in the show ring may alter the appearance of a breed in the space of a few years, but nature's changes are seldom as dramatic. The type of terrier required today to bolt a fox from its earth is the same as it was during the

ABOVE: As far back as the 18th century, there is pictorial evidence of white-bodied terriers.

LEFT: The Jack Russell Terrier takes its name from Parson John Russell, the great hunting enthusiast of the 19th century.

ABOVE: The breed is characterised by its quick wits and fearlessness.

BELOW: The Jack Russell has now been adopted as a favourite family companion.

Reverend John Russell's own lifetime and before. Terriers looking just like Carlisle Tack can still be seen at both Kennel Club shows and Hunt shows alike. However, the decline in blood sports means that fewer terriers are seen today in the field.

OFFICIAL RECOGNITION
In 1990 the Parson Jack Russell Terrier achieved official recognition from the British Kennel Club, and has subsequently achieved recognition from the equivalent bodies in Europe and abroad. For many years prior to recognition, the Jack Russell Terrier has had its faithful band of enthusiasts, with various breed clubs organising their own shows. During this time when there was no official Breed Standard, the Jack Russell deviated in type, and a shorter-legged dog also became popular. This type is still very much in existence today, but is not officially recognised by the British Kennel Club.

In Australia, the Australian National Kennel Council (ANKC) recognises both the Parson Jack Russell Terrier as it is recognised in Britain, and a shorter-legged variation, with Australia being regarded as the country of development for the smaller variety. The 'Australian' Jack Russell Terrier should be between 10-12 inches at the shoulder, making the two varieties quite distinct. They are recognised as two separate breeds and breeding between the two varieties is not allowed. The main difference between the Parson Jack Russell and the 'Australian' Jack Russell Terrier is the obvious difference in the length of leg.

The Parson Jack Russell Terrier is now recognised in a number of countries worldwide from Sweden to South Africa, and the number of Parson Jack Russell Terriers registered with official national bodies continues to grow. In many countries where the Jack Russell is popular, you will find both the short-legged Jack Russell Terrier type and the Parson Jack Russell Terrier, but few countries, other than Australia, officially recognise both varieties. As is the case in Britain, wherever the Jack Russell Terrier is popular it will be supported by its own selection of breed clubs, each with a number of enthusiasts interested in one type or the other.

As official recognition for the breed continues to spread, the number of Jack Russell Terriers seen competing within the mainstream of canine exhibitors increases, as do their accomplishments. The Jack Russell is truly an all-round breed; it is successful in breed competition, at agility and as a working terrier, and it has also gained worldwide popularity as a family pet.

THE BREED STANDARD
The present Breed Standard issued by the Kennel Club for the Parson Jack Russell calls for a dog of similar dimensions to that of a full-grown vixen fox. The ideal height is given as 14 inches (35cms) for a dog, and 13 inches (32.5cms) for a bitch. The colour can be all-white or white with marking of lemon, tan or black, or a combination of these, i.e. tri-colour, with the markings preferably being confined to the head and root of tail. The coat can be rough, broken or smooth, but there should always be a dense, soft undercoat and a harsh, straight top-coat. Ears should be small, V-shaped, carried close to the head and of moderate thickness.

While no mention is made in the Standard of the desired weight, the Jack Russell Terrier should appear balanced in profile, and of a moderate build. The overall impression of the Jack Russell should be one of strength and stamina encompassed within a relatively small frame, but without exaggeration or coarseness.

OWNING A JACK RUSSELL

In temperament, the Jack Russell Terrier should be bold and friendly, with no aggressive or nervous tendencies. He should be biddable and even-tempered while in the presence of other dogs and livestock. Any Jack Russell Terrier used to assist with a pack of hounds in pursuit of their quarry has to be of a sensible and sociable disposition, for he will be expected to mix freely with the hounds, horses, huntsmen and women.

Still used today for its original purpose of bolting foxes and keeping down vermin, the Jack Russell Terrier is an active, alert and intelligent little dog. Full of life and intelligence, the ever-inquisitive Jack Russell will investigate any hedgerow or ditch whenever the opportunity presents itself. This is a dog that needs plenty of exercise and mental stimulation if he is to be kept happy.

Equally at home whether in the town or the country, providing the Jack Russell is properly housed and exercised, he will provide his owner with many years of devoted loyalty and untroubled enjoyment. A hardy terrier, the Jack Russell is free from many of the hereditary afflictions associated with so many of today's pedigree breeds of dog.

However, before embarking on the search for a Jack Russell Terrier, you should be sure it is the breed that you want. It is a terrier, and like all terriers, the Jack Russell has a strong but rewarding personality. This is especially the case since the Jack Russell is still bred as a worker, and retains many of the attributes first bred for in a terrier. The Jack Russell Terrier is a breed with brain, and there is no doubt that he will know how to use that brain to his best advantage. But, handled and trained correctly, the Jack Russell will make an excellent family pet.

Chapter Two

CHOOSING A JACK RUSSELL

FINDING A SUITABLE BREEDER

Having given your choice of breed much consideration, and decided that the Jack Russell Terrier is the breed that you definitely want, you will need to obtain a list of breeders. Your national Kennel Club will be able to supply you with a list of the various breed clubs and their secretaries, who in turn should be able to supply you with a list of breeders, or club members, in your area. Not every club member breeds from their terrier, but most will be more than willing to help you in your search for a puppy. As with many other breeds, all breeders will have certain characteristics unique to their own breeding plans. It is therefore important to see as many examples of the breed as possible in order that you can make a well-informed decision.

ASSESSING THE LITTER

When you visit a breeder, there are many factors to evaluate before getting down to choosing a puppy. The puppies should be kept in a clean environment, and all members of the litter should be clean, bright-eyed and lively. Make sure that you see the mother of the puppies with her litter, along with any other adults

FACING PAGE: It is important to weigh up all the pros and cons of owning a terrier before looking for a puppy.

RIGHT: Ask the breeder about the character of each of the puppies, and try to select the pup that will suit your lifestyle.

that the breeder may have. If possible, you should also try to see the father of the puppies. Some bitches will lose a little condition after whelping, but will never look neglected if they have been properly cared for. Always try to buy a puppy from a reputable breeder who has extended care and attention not only to the rearing of the puppies, but also to any adults he or she may have.

In the search for a reputable breeder, and in turn for a puppy, it is also important not be too influenced by the achievements in the show ring of any particular 'kennel'. The number of wins, if you are interested in them, should always be compared to the number of puppies produced by that breeder, giving a percentage of winning Jack Russell Terriers from the number of puppies bred. In a truly successful 'kennel' the number of puppies produced need not be high for the breeder to make a mark on the show scene.

Unlike tins on a supermarket shelf, puppies are not always conveniently available when you want one. A great many reputable breeders will have a waiting list for puppies, and you may be added to the list. This will allow both the buyer and the seller thinking time to make a well-informed decision, either way, before the puppy is purchased.

TEMPERAMENT
If you are not intending to show your puppy, the prime consideration must be temperament. A dog's character is not, as is sometimes thought, exclusively the result of the owner's rearing and training programme. Temperament is an inherited characteristic, and, while the puppy's experiences may mould the temperament for better or worse, they will only alter the underlying character of the dog in a very minor way. Jack Russell Terrier puppies should always be forthcoming and friendly, and a healthy

puppy will always be bright-eyed and full of life.

Try to pick the type of puppy that will fit in with your lifestyle. If you, for example, have a busy lifestyle with a lot going on, it is best to go for the puppy that is forthcoming, taking everything in his stride. For the quiet person, a very boisterous puppy is not going to make the best companion. Do take time to consider your choice of puppy. Many of the adult Jack Russell Terriers that end up with breed rescue societies do so because they did not suit their owners to begin with.

MALE OR FEMALE
The sex of the puppy is really of little relevance if you are looking for a pet. It is largely a matter of personal preference. If you choose a bitch, you will have to cope with her seasonal cycle, making sure she is kept from male dogs when she is on heat. The male dog may show signs of slightly anti-social behaviour during adolescence, such as 'mounting' legs or cushions, and some adult males have a tendency to wander. Unless you plan to breed, it is advisable to neuter your dog, so that any of the problems commonly associated with either sex will be eliminated. If the intention is to show or breed, it may be better to start off with a bitch, so that, if you become involved in showing, it will be easier to improve on your bitch by taking her to a good stud dog, in the hope that the puppies will improve on any of their mother's faults. You must make your intentions clear so that the breeder can help you to ake the correct choice.

COAT AND COLOUR
The next consideration will have to be any preferences for colour or coat type. Jack Russells may have smooth, broken or rough coats. The colours are tan and white, black and white, and tri-colour,

although white should always predominate. However, most owners attach little importance to coat and colour as the main priority is to find a healthy puppy, with a temperament you like. Remember, this is a decision that you are going to have to live with for the rest of the dog's life – and that will probably be the best part of fifteen years, or perhaps more.

THE PUPPY'S FUTURE

If you have found a reputable breeder, it is well worth listening to his or her advice when it comes to choosing a puppy. The breeder has had the opportunity to observe the puppies closely over a number of weeks, and will have found out about their individual characters, as well as evaluating their conformation. A good breeder will know the puppies and should be able to point new owners towards the most suitable puppy for their lifestyle. With the breeder's advice and knowledge you should be able to make the best choice.

It is important to be clear in your own mind as to what you are looking for. Is your puppy solely to be a pet? Are you likely to be interested in showing or breeding from your puppy when it is older? If you are looking for a puppy of show quality, make this clear to the breeder. Even in the most carefully planned and well-bred litter, there will be some element of variation in quality among the puppies and in their outlook on life. Only the very best specimens should be bred from, and if the potential show dog is to be successful in the show ring, it will need careful choosing. For this reason, it may be better to delay choosing a show puppy until you have some idea as to its potential.

THE OLDER DOG

Sometimes, through no fault of its own, an older dog or young adult may need

re-homing. Before embarking on the search for a puppy, it is a good idea to consider whether an older puppy or an adult Jack Russell Terrier may be more suitable for your circumstances. There are various reasons which could lead to the adult Jack Russell finding himself in need of a new home. It could be the result of a marriage break-up, the owner may have become too ill to care for the dog, or, sometimes, the dog out-lives his owner. In the majority of these cases, the Jack Russell will be of a perfectly suitable disposition for a pet. The advantages of re-homing an adult dog are that there is no need for house-training, the dog will have grown out of his destructive, chewing puppy stage, and the terrier's character and temperament will be fully developed.

It may also be worth considering taking on the older puppy or adolescent. It is common practice among breeders to "run on" the best two or three from the litter until they are six months or so, perhaps even twelve months or more. Such puppies will, more often than not, be of sufficient merit to have warranted being "run on", and although the breeder will be keeping what he believes to be the best puppy, those that are sold subsequently will still be good examples of the breed. This is particularly relevant if your intention is to show the puppy, as its potential as a show dog may not always be easy to assess before the age of six months. By the age of five or six months, the puppy will have his adult dentition, and the mouth can be checked to ensure that the bite is correct for the breed and that the terrier has a full set of teeth.

The advantages of acquiring a puppy at around six months of age are that the puppy will already be fully inoculated, he will probably be house-trained, and he may well have received preliminary training as a show dog and be partially

ABOVE: All members of the litter should appear bright-eyed and lively.

LEFT: It is helpful if you can see some of the adult dogs in the kennel to give you an idea of the type of dog that is being produced.

ABOVE: You can learn a lot by watching puppies play together.

BELOW: It may be that it is more practical to take on an older dog, rather than buying a puppy.

trained as such. Again, he will have outgrown the chewing stage.

It may be that a breeder has a retired brood bitch that he or she wishes to re-home. If a breeder has a number of dogs that are kept in kennels, it is kinder to re-home the older dogs that have fulfilled their purpose, in order that they may then live out the rest of their lives in the comfort of a house as a family pet. Even at nine years old, a Jack Russell Terrier will still have a good few years of life left and this may prove an ideal solution for the elderly owner.

PREPARING FOR THE NEW ARRIVAL

Preparations must be made in advance for the arrival of the new puppy, or the adult Jack Russell Terrier. If you are getting a puppy, both your house and your garden should be made safe. Inside the house, check for trailing electrical flexes, and make sure, as far as possible, that any precious objects are kept out of reach. Make sure the garden is securely fenced, and also check that there are no gaps in the hedges where an inquisitive puppy could crawl through. Before you go to collect the puppy, ask the breeder for a diet sheet so that you will be able to stock up with the type of food to which the puppy has been accustomed. If you have decided to take on an adult Jack Russell Terrier, you should also find out what diet the dog has been accustomed to.

DOG BOWLS

You will need two bowls for your dog; one for drinking water and one for food. The best type to buy are those made of stainless-steel. They are easy to clean and last a lifetime.

BEDS AND CRATES

There are various styles of dog bed on the market, and most will be suitable for the Jack Russell Terrier. However, it is important to remember that puppies are inclined to chew during their teething stage, and any bed bought for the puppy may need to be replaced when the puppy is older. For this reason, it may be advisable to use a cardboard box (ensuring it is free of metal staples) for the first couple of months. This will be perfectly comfortable as long as it is lined with washable bedding material. The bed should be placed in a warm, draught-free corner where the puppy or adult will be able to enjoy some element of privacy.

Crates are becoming increasingly popular, and many dog owners find them invaluable. Although they are expensive, they are virtually indestructible and will provide a 'home' for your dog throughout his life. The advantage of a crate is that the puppy can be confined at night, and for short periods during the day. The puppy soon learns to accept his crate as a safe haven, and will go into it at will. If you stay away from home, the crate can be packed up and taken with you, ensuring that your dog will settle happily in a strange place.

COLLARS AND LEADS

As soon as your puppy has had a chance to settle, he will need to start getting used to wearing a collar. To begin with, this should be soft, perhaps made of rolled leather. Obviously you will need a bigger collar as your puppy grows, but this can be purchased at a later stage. You will also need to have some form of identity disc to attach to the collar.

Your puppy will not be allowed to venture beyond the garden until he has completed his vaccination course, but you can practise lead training in the garden. There is a wide variety of leads to choose from, made from many different materials. It is advisable to start with a light, nylon lead, which the puppy will scarcely notice. When he is bigger, you will probably want to graduate to a leather lead. This is much kinder on the hands, particularly if your puppy has a tendency to pull. Whatever lead you choose, make sure it will be ecure, as the Jak Russell although small, still has considerable strength.

TOYS

Toys need to be provided for both the new puppy and the adult Jack Russell Terrier. There are a great many dog toys available through pet shops and dog shows. While the vast majority will at least provide your pet with some degree of enjoyment, the specially-designed orthodontic toys will aid the puppy with teething and help with the dental care of the adult Jack Russell Terrier. Any toys which your Jack Russell Terrier is going to be left with should be strong and safe.

VACCINATIONS

It is a good idea to consult your veterinary surgery in advance to enquire about the procedure for vaccinating puppies. Puppies need to be vaccinated against parvovirus, leptospirosis and canine hepatitis. The first vaccination is usually given at between eight and ten weeks, and will be followed by a second at least two weeks later. Some practices will also give the puppy a third injection at about the eighteen-week stage. Before your puppy has been fully inoculated he should not be taken beyond your house and garden.

COLLECTING YOUR PUPPY

At last, the big day arrives when you are ready to collect your puppy. If you are travelling by car, it is a good idea to take a friend or a member of the family with you to hold the puppy on the return journey. Take a towel for the puppy to lie on, and some paper towels in case of accidents. Arrange with the breeder to collect your puppy reasonably early in the day, as this will give your puppy time to adapt to his new home before night-time.

When you collect your puppy, the breeder should provide you with a diet sheet (if this has not been sent to you already). Many breeders will supply a small quantity of food so that the puppy does not have to experience any change in diet, no matter how minor, for the first few meals. If you are purchasing a pedigree Parson Jack Russell Terrier, you will need the paperwork from the relevant Kennel Club.

On the journey home, make sure the puppy is held firmly, or confined in a crate. Hopefully, the breeder will not have fed him prior to the journey, and so he should not suffer any ill-effects. Some puppies may salivate or drool when they first travel in a car, and so the paper towels may well come in handy.

ARRIVING HOME

The new puppy has so much to get used to when he first arrives home. Everything is strange, and he has left the security of his mother and his brothers and sisters. To begin with, allow your puppy to explore, first in the garden, and then take him into the kitchen (or wherever he is to sleep). Introduce members of the family in a calm, relaxed manner, and avoid the temptation of inviting all your friends and neighbours to meet the new arrival. If you already have a dog or cat living in the house, introductions must be supervised closely. Make sure that the older dog does not have his nose put out of joint by making too much fuss of the puppy. Equally, it is important to make sure the puppy does not tease the older dog. In most cases, the older dog will give a warning growl, and the puppy will learn to respect him.

Do not be worried if your new puppy refuses to eat the first meal you give him.

LEFT: A crate is an invaluable piece of equipment. In no time, your Jack Russell will regard it as his own safe haven.

BELOW: The Jack Russell is a strong dog for his size, and so you will need a secure collar and lead, preferably made of leather.

The new puppy will have a lot of new things to get used to when he first arrives home.

Jack Russells are inquisitive dogs, and will enjoy new and interesting things to play with and explore – as long as they are safe.

He will be distracted by his new surroundings and will probably not feel settled enough to eat. Make sure he has fresh water to drink – and he will probably make up for his temporary loss of appetite at the next mealtime!

THE FIRST NIGHT

This can be a testing time for both puppy and owner. The best course of action is to settle your puppy in his bed or crate, and close the door on him. Nearly all puppies will make a fuss at being left. They miss the warmth and companionship of their littermates, and they have yet to settle into their new home. Make the bed as comfortable as possible, with an old toy to snuggle up to (making sure the eyes or any other potentially dangerous parts have been removed). You could also provide a covered hot-water bottle to keep the puppy warm. However, your puppy will almost certainly voice his protests, and it is just a matter of leaving him to it. In fact, he will be so tired after his traumatic day, he will settle down to sleep, eventually.

It is very tempting to go and comfort your bewildered little puppy, but you could be making a rod for your own back. If your puppy learns that a loud protest on his part results in attention from you, he will continue to cry every night. If you are deaf to his cries, he will soon learn to settle down to sleep.

HOUSE-TRAINING

Ideally, your puppy should be kept indoors and encouraged to use newspapers as a start to house-training. The newspapers should be placed near to the door, and each time the puppy awakens, and following each meal, he should be placed on the newspapers and encouraged to use them. Every time the puppy uses the newspapers, he should be praised. Most puppies will soon get the idea. The next stage is to get the puppy used to relieving himself in the garden. This transition is perfectly straightforward if you always take the puppy out after meals and on waking, and go to the same spot in the garden. It is a good idea to use a command such as "Be Clean" and say it every time the puppy performs. It will not be long before the pup associates the word with the correct response.

Similarly, if you have taken on an older dog that has been used to living in a kennel, he may need time to adjust to living in the house. However, the adult dog will be quicker in grasping what is required and will not take long to adapt to a new regime.

Chapter Three

CARING FOR YOUR JACK RUSSELL

FEEDING

Nutritional requirement should be one of the main considerations for the Jack Russell owner, particularly during the vital growing period. It is absolutely essential that a puppy receives an adequate diet, to ensure correct and healthy development of the teeth, bones, skin, muscles and coat. In order that any deficiencies be avoided, it is probably best to feed your puppy on a good-quality proprietary brand of pet food designed especially for the puppy or junior stages of growth. When feeding a 'complete' diet, make sure that fresh drinking water is available at all times. If the decision is taken to feed the growing Jack Russell Terrier on fresh meat, then the use of a supplement for puppies and growing dogs will be necessary.

As the puppy develops, he will not want as many small meals spaced throughout the day. Most puppies start with four meals a day from eight weeks of age, often divided between meat and cereal feeds. By twelve weeks of age, this can be reduced to three meals. By the time he is five to six months old, he may well start leaving some of his midday meal, and so the ration can be reduced to two meals a day. He should continue on two meals a day until he reaches the age of eleven or twelve months. At this stage, your Jack Russell Terrier can have the feeding routine reduced to one meal a day, fed either in the morning or evening.

WORMING

Until the age of six months, your puppy will need to be treated for the roundworm, *Toxocara Canis*, with a suitable compound, taking care to follow the manufacturer's instructions for administration. When your puppy receives his initial vaccinations at eight to twelve weeks, you can ask your vet to recommend a worming programme. The puppy should be wormed again at six months (this should be an all-purpose worm treatment which also eliminates tapeworm, *Dipylidium caninum*), and then routinely following your vet's advice.

TEETHING

The 'puppy teeth' will begin to fall out from as early as twelve weeks, starting with the middle incisors. The deciduous teeth will be replaced by the adult teeth over a period of two or three months. This seldom causes any problems, but the puppy should be checked to make sure all the deciduous teeth have actually come out. Sometimes the adult canine teeth will fail to push the 'puppy' canine out, resulting in 'double' teeth. However, if the puppy is encouraged to chew on hard biscuits and chew-sticks, this should help the teeth to come out.

If any of the deciduous teeth have not fallen out by the time your Jack Russell has reached the age of eleven months or so, then they may need to be removed

It is essential that your puppy receives a well-balanced diet while he is growing.

Providing chew-sticks will help your puppy when he is teething.

The adult Jack Russell Terrier is an **inquisitive** *and energetic dog who will love investigating new walks.*

FACING PAGE: In the first few months, your puppy will derive most of his exercise from playing.

under anaesthetic by your vet. If the puppy teeth are left, they are likely to harbour trapped particles of food and cause damage to the adult tooth.

SOCIALISATION
This is possibly the most vital part of a puppy's all-round education. In the first twelve months, you should ensure that your Jack Russell encounters as many different experiences as possible. This may involve a great many short walks in busy streets while the puppy is still young, in order to accustom him to traffic and to people. If you do not have children in the family, make sure he has the opportunity to play with some youngsters who are used to dogs. He should also meet other dogs, and get used to other livestock. A puppy that is carefully socialised will give the owner few problems when he is an adult. Take care when introducing your puppy to other dogs, ensuring that the other dog is friendly. A bad experience at an early age could reflect on his outlook later in life.

EXERCISE
Exercise for the young puppy should be limited, as the puppy needs time to develop physically before being given the rigorous exercise enjoyed by many adult Jack Russell Terriers. It will be obvious when the youngster is showing signs of tiring, and this is the time to curtail exercise. The adult Jack Russell thrives on exercise. He is a lively, inquisitive, agile little dog, and will enjoy investigating new walks whenever possible. However, make sure you know the areas well, as the Jack Russell is still led by his instinct, and there is always a danger that he may attempt to 'go to ground' and then become trapped.

A CARE ROUTINE
Grooming is an essential part of caring

for your Jack Russell. The main purpose is to keep his coat clean and in good condition, but it also gives the opportunity to examine your dog on a regular basis. In this way you will be able to spot any signs of trouble at the earliest stage – and so any treatment required is likely to be more successful.

TEETH
On a weekly basis, your Jack Russell Terrier should have his teeth and gums examined for signs of tartar build-up, damage to the dentition, and gum disease. There are various products available to help keep the terrier's teeth in good order, without the assistance of the owner. These range from specially designed tug-toys to chew-sticks shaped for maximum dental benefit. Bones can help reduce tartar on the teeth but, if the terrier is an enthusiastic bone chewer, they may actually do more damage to the teeth than good.

If necessary, the Jack Russell's teeth should be cleaned with a toothpaste and toothbrush designed for canine use. The toothpaste will usually be of a more acceptable flavour to the dog than the human equivalents. If the tartar is allowed to build up it may become necessary for the dog to have his teeth scaled and polished, and, in extreme cases, or where there is damage to the teeth, some may need to be removed. This is usually performed by a veterinarian while the dog is under anaesthetic. Particular attention should be paid to the carnasial teeth at the back of the dog's mouth for signs of damage. These are more likely to have sustained damage, perhaps from chewing on bones or from pulling at roots if the terrier is an enthusiastic digger. Gums also need to be checked for any signs of gum disease. The healthy gums of an adult Jack Russell will either be pink or dark, depending on the pigmentation.

EARS

The ears also need to be checked regularly and, if necessary, cleaned using a proprietary aural cleansing fluid and cotton-wool. Be careful not to probe inside the ear, as you could do serious damage. Limit cleaning to the area that is visible. The use of an aural cleansing solution will help bring any dirt and wax from deeper within the ear to the surface so that it can be cleaned effectively. Cleansing fluid will be sufficient if there is only a build-up of wax or dirt, but if the ears have become infested with ear mites, treatment will be needed using insecticidal ear-drops.

Ear mites will cause the dog quite a lot of distress, with the dog frequently shaking his head and scratching at the ears, often whimpering at the same time. Veterinary advice should be sought to ensure that treatment with the insecticidal ear-drops is appropriate, and that the cause of the problem is not more serious, such as a grass seed in the ear canal.

EYES

The eyes must be kept free from dirt. Each day the inner corner of the eye should be carefully wiped with a damp ball of cotton-wool. The main causes of eye infection are usually dirt that has got into the eye, or a draught where the terrier has been sleeping. Occasionally a terrier may have a foreign object in his eye which may or may not cause distress. Likewise, the foreign object may or may not be visible to the owner. If a weeping eye has not cleared up within a couple of days then veterinary advice should be sought without delay. Often the eye-rim will become damaged and this will also cause the eye to weep. The lifestyle of the Jack Russell and his love of crawling through bushes and undergrowth means it is quite common for the terrier to sustain damage to the eyes. If

professional advice is sought without delay the damage is likely to have little or no lasting ill effect.

NAILS AND FEET

Nails should be checked regularly to see if they need to be trimmed. If your Jack Russell is exercised regularly on hard surfaces, and the feet are of the correct shape, the nails should not need to be trimmed. However, incorrect feet, or inadequate exercise on hard ground, may mean that the dog's nails will need to be cut from time to time. If you are not confident about cutting the nails yourself, then ask your vet or someone who has plenty of experience. The dog has a quick on each nail, and if it is cut, it will bleed profusely. A bad experience will mean that your Jack Russell will be very reluctant to have his nails trimmed in the future.

The nails will either be pink, in which case the quick is visible, or they may be black, when, obviously, the quick cannot be seen. Some Jack Russells will have nails of both colours, in which case it is best to start with the pink ones. The nail should be cut a little below the quick with suitable nail-clippers, such as the guillotine type. In the majority of cases, it will only be the middle two nails on the front feet that require cutting – unless the terrier has had very little walking on hard surfaces.

The skin around the top of the nails also needs to be checked for signs of infection. If the skin around the base of the nail appears red or swollen, the foot should be bathed in a solution of salt water. If the pad looks particularly red or swollen, seek veterinary advice. Often problems with feet occur when the terrier does a lot of running on hard ground, or frequently digs in the earth.

During the summer months, check the feet regularly for signs of grass seeds between the toes. If these go unnoticed,

The Jack Russell should be accustomed to grooming and handling from an early age.

If nails need to be trimmed, the guillotine type of nail-clippers should be used.

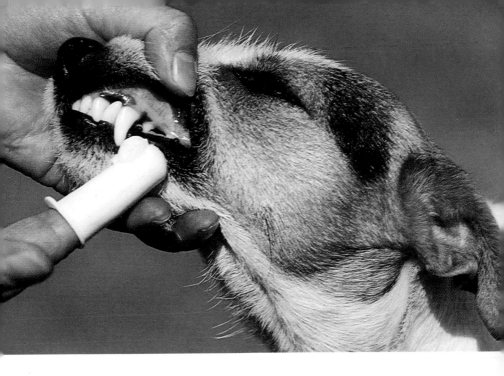

ABOVE: Teeth can be cleaned using a finger-brush.

BELOW: Some owners find it easier to use a toothbrush when cleaning the teeth.

they can cause an abscess. Similarly, the underside of the pads also need to be checked for grass seeds. Pads can become cracked or split, usually resulting in lameness. This needs to checked to ensure that the lameness is not being caused by a foreign object which has penetrated the pad. If in any doubt, then contact your veterinary surgeon who will be able to give you the best advice.

GROOMING YOUR JACK RUSSELL TERRIER

CORRECT COAT AND TEXTURE
The amount of grooming that your Jack Russell Terrier will require will depend on his coat type. The Jack Russell Terrier's coat essentially comes in three varieties: the smooth-coated Russell, the broken-coated Russell and the rough-coated Russell. In all three varieties, the coat should consist of an undercoat and a top-coat. The top-coat will vary in length depending on the coat type, but the undercoat should always be the same – short, soft and very dense. The top-coat should be hard and straight, ideally lying flat to the body, giving good protection from the elements. The Reverend Thomas Pearce, writing in the 1870s, describes the coat of his terrier, which was bred by the Reverend John Russell.
"It is rather long, very hard or harsh, and yet perfectly smooth; his legs are clean, and the whole profile of the dog is sharp and defined."
The reference would, by no means, be referring to a terrier that had been stripped. The terrier would have been in its natural state, given the period in which the statement was made. The Russell coat should never be confused with the profuse coat of the present-day Wire Fox Terriers, nor should it need as much stripping. In 1872 the Reverend Pearce wrote:

"The peculiar texture does not interfere with the profile of the body, though there is a shaggy eyebrow and a pronounced moustache. The eyebrow is a great mark, giving the dog the look of a Bristol merchant."
Obviously, the smooth-coated Jack Russell will lack the characteristic eyebrows and moustache, but this makes the smooth-coated Russell no less correct in breed type. The eyebrows and moustache should grow naturally and should not need to be the result of skilful trimming.

GROOMING REQUIREMENTS
A good Jack Russell coat should only need brushing to keep it clean. The natural oils present in the coat should act as a repellent to dirt and water, keeping the terrier's skin dry should he find himself out in the rain. Although the Jack Russell should be groomed regularly throughout the year, whether smooth, broken, or rough-coated, he will require more grooming in the spring of each year. Grooming should become part of a regular routine and presents the owner with an ideal opportunity to check the terrier for signs of parasites such as fleas. During the regular grooming sessions any long hairs that grow upwards from in front of the eyes should be removed. This is done by gripping the hair between your finger and thumb and pulling it out.
In spring the Jack Russell Terrier will begin to shed his winter coat, resulting in an increase in the amount of hair found around the house and in the dog's sleeping quarters. If the Jack Russell has a smooth coat, there will be no coat to strip out and grooming is relatively simple. Using a slicker-brush, the coat should be brushed against the pattern of growth to remove any loose hair and dead undercoat. The dead undercoat will appear in the brush as soft, downy hair.

Do not use a slicker-brush that is too hard, as this will scratch the dog's skin and will make grooming an unpleasant experience.

After removing the dead undercoat, the top-coat should be rubbed with a damp cloth, or damp hands, first against the pattern of growth, and then with the direction of growth. This should remove the loose top-coat. However, the process may need to be repeated a number of times before the terrier has finished shedding his coat.

HAND-STRIPPING
In the spring, the broken, or rough-coated, Jack Russell will need to be stripped out by hand. Without stripping, the coat will fall out in time anyway, but if it is all stripped out at once it will grow in more neatly, and there will be less hair left lying around the house. There is no need to bath the dog prior to stripping, though it will do no harm to wash the dog after he has been stripped.

A STEP BY STEP GUIDE
The coat should be prepared in the same manner as the smooth-coated Jack Russell, using the slicker-brush. The loose undercoat will be removed with the slicker-brush, but the top-coat will need to be removed by hand.

Start at the back of the neck and, using your finger and thumb, grip the hair near the base. Pull the hair away from the dog in the direction that it is growing, making sure you do not pull out the undercoat. If the coat is ready to come out, this should require little effort on the part of the owner – and it will not hurt the dog. If the coat does not come away when pulled, it may not yet be ready to be stripped and should be left for another week or so.

Providing the terrier's coat is coming out easily, continue to pull out the hair from the back of the neck, always pulling

in the direction of the growth. Continue over the shoulders, along the back, and towards the tail. The coat will be heavier around the neck and over the shoulders if your Jack Russell has the correct coat. When you have removed all the hair from the neck and the back, the hair under the throat and down the tummy will need to be removed. If the growth on the undersides is quite heavy, it may be better to do it a little at a time. If the process is proving to be very time-consuming, it can be done over a couple of days.

For neatness, any long hairs on the underside of the tail should be removed, using finger and thumb. Also check for any straggling hairs that may interfere with the profile of the dog. Use a small pair of sharp scissors to trim the hair around the genitalia. Scissors can also be used to cut any long hairs around the outside edges of the feet. Do not trim over the top of the feet or the nails, as you will leave unsightly scissor marks. It is important to keep a pair of scissors specifically for trimming your Jack Russell's coat. Ideally, these should be small, round-ended scissors, specifically designed for trimming dogs. These can be bought at trade stands at the bigger dog shows, at large pet stores, or from grooming parlours. It is important to have good scissors, and it is also important to keep them sharp. Blunt scissors leave a poor finish, and they are also more likely to contribute to making errors.

Once the broken, or rough-coated Jack Russell has been stripped out, he will resemble the smooth-coated variety. A new coat will begin to grow through about six weeks or so after the dog has been stripped, but it may be a good few months before the dog has regained his full coat. If your Jack Russell Terrier has an extremely heavy coat, or a particularly soft coat, it may not be suitable for

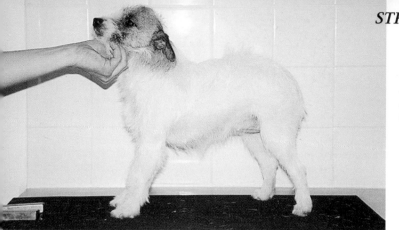

An untrimmed
Jack Russell in
need of stripping.

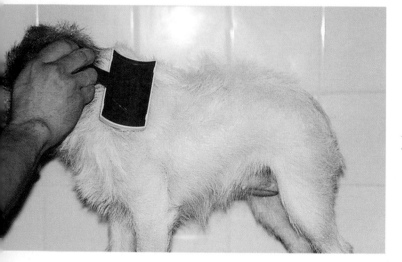

Brush the coat
thoroughly using
a slicker-brush
against the
pattern of
growth.

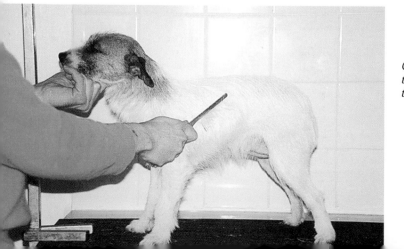

Comb the coat
through
thoroughly.

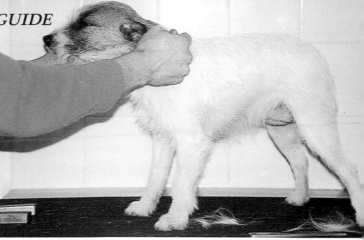

Using finger and thumb, start stripping out the long hairs.

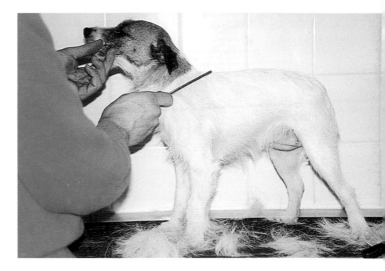

Use the comb against the pattern of growth to show the long hairs.

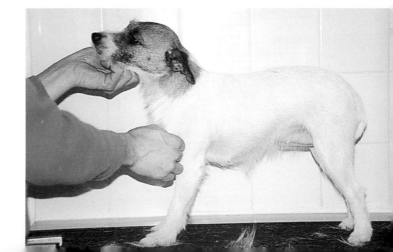

Pull out the long hairs.

stripping. If in doubt, seek the advice of someone with experience of grooming who can assess your dog's coat for you.

GROOMING FOR THE SHOW RING

The Jack Russell Terrier should never require specialised trimming for the show ring. A little more attention to detail is all that is needed.

If the coat has begun to shed, it will need to be stripped out totally by hand. Once the new coat begins to grow through, the terrier should have any remaining long hairs stripped out, paying particular attention to the profile of the dog. The neck should be carefully stripped out to give a neat outline. Any long hairs on the head, growing between the ears, will need to be removed to give the skull the appearance of being flat. The ears should not require any trimming if the coat is correct. Any long hairs along the tummy should be trimmed to give a neat outline. The same applies to the hair on the feet and under the tail. Once the top-coat has grown through a little, and the harsh texture of the coat is evident, the terrier is ready for competition.

The process of removing any stray, long hairs from the back and shoulders, and enhancing the outline of the terrier, should be repeated every few weeks while the Jack Russell is continuing to be shown. Do not bath your Jack Russell prior to going to a show, unless it is really necessary, as this will alter the natural texture of the coat.

BATHING YOUR JACK RUSSELL

A good, correct Jack Russell Terrier coat, whether smooth, broken or rough, does not need to be bathed in order to remove everyday dirt. The natural oils in the coat should ensure that any mud and dirt that the terrier picks up when out walking will drop off when dry. Brushing with a good-quality slicker-brush should be all that is required to restore the coat's whiteness.

Of course, not all dirt and mud is odourless – and sometimes you may find that your Jack Russell has been in contact with something unpleasant and foul-smelling! In this case, bathing may be necessary to remove the unpleasant odour.

It is important when bathing any dog that the temperature of the water is not too high. Lukewarm is hot enough. Use a good-quality, mild dog shampoo that is unlikely to irritate the skin, and follow the manufacturer's instructions before the dog is put into the bath. Remember to have dry towels on hand. If possible, shower the dog as this is swift and effective, and the dog does not have to stand in any depth of water.

Leaving the head dry to begin with, soak the dog's body and then apply the shampoo, working it into the coat, all over the body. Rinse the body throughout. Next, wet the head and apply shampoo, taking care to avoid the eyes and nostrils. All shampoo must be thoroughly rinsed off before the dog is dried. A correct Jack Russell coat will consist of a soft, dense undercoat and a harsh top-coat. The undercoat, once wet, will take some time to dry out completely, and unless the weather is fine, your Jack Russell will need to be kept inside for a couple of hours until he is thoroughly dry.

THE ELDERLY JACK RUSSELL

Most Jack Russell Terriers will keep in good health as they grow older. The average age of a Jack Russell is about fifteen years, with many reaching eighteen and sometimes twenty years old while still in good health. The Jack Russell bitch who is used for breeding will have had her last litter by the time she is about eight years old. Most national Kennel Clubs have regulations stipulating the age at which pedigree bitches should be retired from breeding. The male Jack Russell will continue to breed for as long as he is able, though his sperm count may become lower as he becomes older, and some of the bitches he mates may fail to conceive.

The weight of the veteran Jack Russell will need to be more carefully monitored as a veteran will be more inclined to put on weight, and it is harder to get the weight back off again. The best practice is to change the dog's diet to a suitable alternative for the ageing dog. Some of the pet food ranges will offer a 'senior' variety. However, most Russells do remain quite active as they age, and this must also be reflected in the dog's diet. If your Russell is gaining weight easily and you are having problems keeping the weight down, then this is an indication that it may be time to change the diet.

The teeth of the veteran Russell will need to be checked more regularly for signs of decay and damage, particularly to the carnasial teeth at the back of the mouth. During grooming, the dog should be checked for any growths or warts. In the bitch, particularly the maiden bitch that is not neutered, the teats should be checked regularly for any signs of mammary tumours. The mammary tumours will manifest themselves as small lumps around the teats. If you discover anything of this nature, ask your vet for advice.

In the veteran male Russell, the testicles should be checked regularly for any abnormalities. Both the testicles should be about the same size; if one feels hard and enlarged, the vet should again be consulted as to the best course of action for the owner to take. Testicular cancer occurs in dogs from time to time and will usually be treated by the removal of the affected testicle, or of both the testicles, i.e. castration.

Exercise for the veteran Jack Russell

Terrier should not necessarily be restricted just because of age, providing the terrier is still keen to go for walks. As your Jack Russell Terrier becomes older, he will normally take less exercise. However, regular daily exercise will help maintain good health. If the terrier appears tired by the amount of exercise he is being given, then the exercise needs to be reduced accordingly.

In general, more attention should be paid during the cleaning of the eyes, ears, etc. for, in most cases, early diagnosis will ensure that any problem is rectified successfully. Any lumps or growths should be checked regularly and the size noted, so that if there is a sudden increase in size, this will be noticed at once and the appropriate action taken.

THE FINAL PARTING
Unfortunately dogs do not live as long as humans, and losing a beloved companion is an inevitable part of dog ownership. In the majority of cases, dogs do not die naturally. We can intervene to put an end to suffering, and this is often the best course of action to take.

It is, without doubt, the hardest decision a dog owner has to face, but it should be viewed as part of the responsibility of caring for a dog. If your Jack Russell has got to the point when he is in pain and has lost his quality of life, it is time to put him to sleep.

Ideally, you should ask the vet to come to your house, so your dog does not have the trauma of going to the surgery. The injection is swift and painless, and your old friend can be eased out of this life while being stroked and comforted in familiar surroundings.

Of course you will miss your old dog, but, in time, you will be able to look back on all the happy times you spent together, knowing that you allowed him a dignified and peaceful end to his life.

STRIPPING: A STEP-BY-STEP GUIDE

Scissors are used to remove the long hairs from around the feet.

Remove the long hairs from under the eyes.

BELOW: The finished strip.

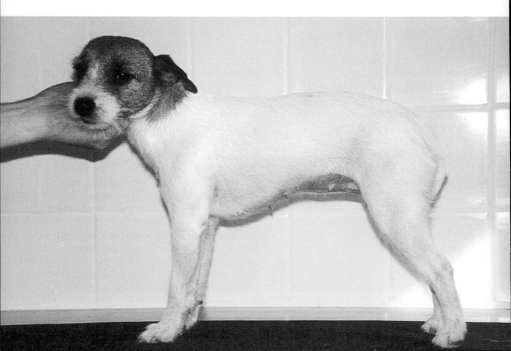

Chapter Four

TRAINING YOUR JACK RUSSELL

KEEP IT SIMPLE

As with any breed, praise is an important aspect of successful training. Most dogs will be eager to please their owners to some degree, and it is this aspect of the dog's nature that the owner must take advantage of during training at all levels. The importance of keeping commands short and simple must also be stressed, as this is the key to success. The dog's understanding of human vocabulary is very limited and, although some dogs do show remarkable intelligence, your pet is unlikely to understand long-winded commands and sentences.

There are some basic commands which should be taught, which are essential to owning a well-behaved and socially acceptable pet. If your dog is off the lead you should be able to recall him when you want to. In public, your Jack Russell should walk at heel on the lead without pulling. He should also remain calm in the face of distractions. While serious

training should not really begin until about six months of age, the way you have reared and socialised your puppy prior to this will have a bearing on how he reacts to noise and other distractions. It is important to introduce your puppy to the noise of traffic and the hurly-burly of the outside world as soon as he is vaccinated. Even if you carry your puppy, he will still be learning. This stage of socialisation is vital for all puppies, and most particularly if you live in town and your puppy is going to be exercised in public parks or walked on the road.

TRAINING EXERCISES

It is essential for both owner and dog to be in a relaxed frame of mind during training sessions if the exercise is to be successful. Try to avoid training when your puppy is likely to be hungry, or amid other such distractions that are likely to result in your Jack Russell Terrier's mind being elsewhere.

LEAD TRAINING

The first task is to introduce your puppy to wearing a collar. Wait until he has settled into his new home, and then try putting on a soft, leather collar. Make sure you have a toy close at hand so you can distract his attention when he starts to scratch at it. In most cases, the puppy will soon forget he is wearing the collar. Leave it on for a short while, and then try again the next day. Gradually extend the time the puppy is wearing his collar until you can leave it on full-time.

The same principles apply when starting lead training. A toy will be useful for distracting the puppy, or you can ask someone to call his name, and then run with him when he responds. To begin with, allow the puppy to go where he wants to go. Never yank or pull your puppy, or he will soon regard the lead as a form of punishment. Build up your lead training with short walks in the garden. By the time your puppy has completed his vaccinations, he will be ready to walk out confidently on the lead.

THE SIT

When you begin teaching this exercise, it will be helpful to keep your Jack Russell Terrier on the lead. Holding the lead in one hand, give the command "Sit" while gently but firmly pressing down on the dog's hindquarters with the other hand. Your puppy will be eased into the Sit, and he should be kept in position for a few seconds. Give the dog plenty of praise and release him. Repeat the exercise two or three times within a short period, but do not allow the exercise to become tedious.

You can reinforce the Sit command at mealtimes by holding the puppy's bowl just above his head. As he looks up he will naturally go into the Sit position. As he does this, give the command "Sit" and place his meal in front of him. If you are using tidbits as a training aid, you can follow the same procedure, holding a tidbit just above your puppy's head, and then rewarding him when he responds correctly.

Follow the same procedure each day and it will not be long before your Jack Russell Terrier responds instantly to the command.

THE DOWN

This is a particularly useful command for your Jack Russell Terrier to understand, and one that you will probably find yourself using most frequently. The Jack Russell is an inquisitive breed and an extremely agile little dog. Most will need to be told to stop jumping up to see what is going on. However, it is important to remember that your dog has only a limited understanding of human vocabulary, and, to begin with, he will not understand that the same command can be applied in different contexts. If your Jack Russell Terrier is inclined to clamber all over furniture, you should use a command that cannot be confused with one used for a different exercise. Of course, the context in which the command is given is of no relevance to your dog. Each command should be specific to one particular exercise, thus avoiding confusion.

To teach your puppy to lie down on command, first put the dog in the sitting position. Keep hold of the lead, and gently but firmly push down on the shoulder blades with one hand, while repeating the word "Down", or whichever word you have decided to use for this exercise. Once your Jack Russell is in the correct position, he should be praised and then allowed to relax. Repeat the exercise once or twice again after about five minutes or so, and end the training session with plenty of praise. It is very important that your puppy does not become bored during training. The exercises should be fun to learn and rewarded with praise.

THE RECALL
Initially, it may be of some benefit to the new owner if you have a friend or a member of the family to assist with the Recall exercise. At the very least, you will need a good length of rope if your Jack Russell Terrier is to be prevented from taking some extra free exercise. Make sure that the environment you choose for training is free from distractions and from any possible hazards.

To begin with, put your Jack Russell in a comfortable position such as the Sit. Using your hand to back up the command "Stay", step back two or three paces from your puppy, with your helper holding on to the lead, or keeping hold with a length of rope tied to the collar. Keep repeating the command. Without exciting your dog too much, encourage

him to come to you and then give plenty of praise. The distance you can leave your puppy can be increased as he becomes familiar with the command.

If your Jack Russell makes a bid for freedom as you step back, put him back in the same position, and repeat the exercise. If he keeps breaking the Stay, it is better to stop, have a game, and then try a simple exercise, such as Sit, where success can be guaranteed. End the training session on a positive note, and try the Recall exercise the following day when, hopefully, your puppy will be in a more responsive frame of mind. Never nag at your Jack Russell, thinking that you must 'win' the battle. You will get far better results if you keep training light-hearted, interspersing exercises with games and with praise.

THE RETRIEVE
The gundog breeds, such as Labrador Retrievers and Golden Retrievers, are bred to retrieve, and they will need very little encouragement before they are retrieving everything in sight! However, this is not the case with the Jack Russell, and so the use of tidbits will be necessary at some times. However, try where possible to accustom your puppy to receiving praise as a reward for good behaviour, rather than food – for you may not always have food on hand to encourage good behaviour.

The retrieve exercise is probably the most difficult exercise for the novice owner to teach. The vast majority of Jack Russells will enjoy chasing a moving object, and this must form the basis of teaching the retrieve. If your puppy is interested in chasing a ball, or any other toy, the only additional element is to teach him to bring the object back to you. Introduce the command "Fetch" when you throw the toy and as your puppy runs out after it. Keep repeating the command as your puppy returns to

Teach your dog to sit by applying gentle pressure to the hindquarters and easing him into position.

The Stay exercise should be built up gradually, leaving your dog for just a few paces to begin with.

To teach the Down, press on the shoulders while giving the command "Down."

When your dog goes into the Down, hold him in position for a few seconds, giving plenty of praise.

you, but do not distract him too much, otherwise he will drop what he is carrying. Once your puppy has returned to you with the desired object, he should be praised, and then throw the object for him again. In this way, the exercise becomes a game which the dog will enjoy, which will make him enthusiastic to respond to the retrieve command on all occasions.

PROBLEM BEHAVIOUR
As with any breed, problems may arise with an individual Jack Russell Terrier resulting from temperament and behaviour. Problems may vary depending on the lifestyle, environment and age of the individual concerned. Behavioural problems may be of a basic nature, as seen in many dogs from a variety of breeds, or they may be more serious and deep-rooted, possibly resulting from the terrier's breeding.

AGGRESSION
Aggression in the individual dog can manifest itself in many ways. When the aggression is directed towards other dogs it may be territorial, which is more likely in the male Jack Russell – and particularly common in the male Jack Russell that has been used for breeding. Aggressive behaviour towards other dogs can also be the result of fear. If your Jack Russell lacks confidence, he may well attempt to 'bluster it out' with other dogs. Fortunately, this type of nervousness can often be overcome. The best course of action is to take your Jack Russell to training classes where he will meet other dogs, and gradually become more confident. This is also relevant if your Jack Russell shows nervousness when approached by people. The more he meets people in controlled situations, the more likely he is to overcome his fears.
Territorial aggression can be solved by

neutering, if the animal is not used for breeding. In the majority of cases, this will alleviate the problem considerably. Territorial aggression can be a problem in a busy household with frequent visitors. If this is the case, it is advisable to keep the dog in a separate room or in his crate, until the visitor is in the house. The dog can then be introduced calmly, and he will not feel so threatened as when greeting strangers on the doorstep.
It is important that you remain calm and confident, despite any aggressive tendencies displayed by your dog. For, more often than not, it is the owner's behaviour that lies at the root of the problem. If the dog senses fear in his owner, then his response will be to defend his owner. Unchecked, the dog will take the 'appropriate' action towards whatever he sees as being the threat. This scenario often becomes a vicous circle in which the owner becomes more tense and apprehensive as another dog approaches, and the terrier becomes more intent on defending his owner.
Training classes will often help alleviate the problem, although, this time, it is the owner who will have to overcome his or her fears, so that the dog will moderate his behaviour. Remember, whenever there is a problem, it is imperative to look carefully at the whole situation, including the dog's background and upbringing, in order that the problem can be dealt with.

DOUBLE TROUBLE
Aggression between two or more Jack Russell Terriers in the same household can become a terrible problem for the owner. If there are bitches and dogs kept in the same household, aggression may develop between the males when the bitches are in season. This may or may not rectify itself when the bitches go out of season, but sometimes the dogs' dislike for each other may become quite

intense. If the problem is dealt with before it is allowed to get to this stage, severe animosity can be avoided. The dogs should be separated when the bitches are in season, and if any of the adults – dog or bitch – are not being used for breeding, they should be neutered.

Once an intense dislike has developed between two dogs, they will seldom become reconciled. In this situation, it is advisable to keep the dogs separate at all times, or to re-home one of them. Bitches may also display aggression towards each other at different stages of their oestrus cycle. However, providing they are of a good temperament, they will settle down once their hormones have returned to normal. If any of the bitches concerned are not being bred from, it is best to have them neutered.

If two Jack Russell Terriers become engaged in battle, it is so important that the owner remains as calm as possible. The terriers should not be pulled apart if they have a good grip on each other, which will often be the case. If possible, immerse the pair in water or throw water in their faces. Most fights between two dogs will seldom become very serious, and it is often possible to separate the two by shouting at them and asserting your own position as the 'pack leader'.

AGGRESSION TOWARDS PEOPLE

A dog who shows aggression towards people can pose a considerable threat – and, in many cases, this deviant behaviour is directed towards the dog's owner. Incorrect training will usually be the root of such a problem, as the Jack Russell has a misplaced sense of dominance over his owner, and the owner – who may be afraid of the dog – has failed to rectify the problem. Once established, this can be a difficult problem to resolve. The best course of action is to enrol in training classes for

the benefit of both dog and owner.

GOING 'AWOL'

The Jack Russell's love of hunting can lead him into mischief. Sometimes he will run off into bushes and fail to return when called. Some terriers will remain there for quite some time. If the dog fails to come after he has been trained, on future occasions he should remain on the lead, and only be allowed to run free in suitable 'distraction-free' environments.

If your Jack Russell wanders away from home, as can be the case with some male Jack Russells in search of bitches in season, the problem will be rectified by neutering. A straying dog causes problems not only for the owner, but also to the general public and other dog owners.

CHEWING

Chewing is most commonly the result of boredom, except during a puppy's teething stages. If a Jack Russell is likely to be left for some time without human company, it may be an idea to purchase another dog to keep the dog company in the absence of the owner. However, two dogs can get up to more mischief than one, so they must be provided with their own toys. The Jack Russell Terrier that likes to chew, even when it has company, needs further training and his own selection of toys.

BASIC DISOBEDIENCE

Basic disobedience is usually the result of inappropriate training, perhaps as a result of the owner's ignorance. Training classes will help to train the dog correctly, or, more precisely, to train the owner. Remember that training classes are there to assist with problem dogs, so no matter how embarrassing it may be trying to work with a disobedient dog, it is worth persevering. Providing you listen to the advice given, and train your

ABOVE: If your puppy is socialised from an early age, experiencing a variety of different situations, he will grow into a well-adjusted adult.

BELOW: Think carefully before taking on two Jack Russell Terriers, you may find that you end up with double trouble!

RIGHT: Basic disobedience is often the result of incorrect training.

BELOW: In all situations, it is a good idea to take your dog to training classes – and then any problems with behaviour can be nipped in the bud.

dog at home as well as at the training
class, you will achieve your goal
eventually. Training classes are there to
assist with any problems you may have
and to teach you the correct way in
which to train your dog. The trainer will
not train your dog for you – that is your
job.

THE CASE FOR NEUTERING

There is no doubt that neutering for the
male Jack Russell will solve a multitude
of problems including leg-lifting around
the house, mounting people's legs, and
aggression towards other dogs. In the
bitch, neutering will solve temperamental
problems that may arise from oestrus-
orientated hormonal changes, such as
those that arise during a false pregnancy.
It also puts a stop to the presence of
stray dogs at the door when the bitch is
in season. Neutered animals are generally
more settled and easier to control than
un-neutered animals.

THE JACK RUSSELL AS A
WORKING TERRIER

It is the Jack Russell attributes as a
working terrier that have ensured his
survival for more than 200 years as a
unique type of terrier. Originally bred to
bolt the fox from its earth, the Jack
Russell Terrier is extremely versatile and
can be used for a number of other
purposes.

BOLTING FOXES

An important aspect concerning
temperament is that the Jack Russell was
not bred to kill the fox, only to bolt it
from its earth – and the dog should
never show signs of needless aggression.
If a fox goes to ground and fails to bolt
after the Jak Russell has entered the
earth, it should be possible for the
terrierman to pinpoint the position of
the fox below ground. Having located
the position of the fox by listening for

the sound of the yapping terrier, the
terrierman can then begin the task of
digging down to the fox. When the fox
is reached, it will be removed. It may be
relocated in a more suitable area, or, if
this is not possible, the fox will have to
be destroyed – an act that the Jack
Russell Terrier will play no part in.

Where the terrain makes digging down
to a fox impossible, the task in hand will
require a different sort of terrier of a
more severe disposition. The Lakeland
Terrier is such a terrier. It was originally
bred to work in the rocky earths of the
Lake District where it would be
impossible to dig down to the fox, and
so would normally be required to dispose
of the fox below ground. The
temperament of such a terrier is quite
different to that of the Jack Russell, who
would normally only be required for the
purpose of assisting with a hunt, i.e. with
Foxhounds – and not to end it.

Another important characteristic of the
Jack Russell Terrier is that an element of
self-control is essential. Although, for the
main part, the training will influence the
terrier's ability to bolt foxes, the dog
must firstly be trainable, and also have
some self-control. The terrier that is used
to bolt foxes will have to ignore
distractions when below ground, such as
the smell of rabbit, or even the presence
of a rabbit in a tight corner. If a
terrierman has spent a considerable
amount of time and expended a lot of
energy in digging down to his dog, he
would be understandably annoyed to
find his dog has been marking a rabbit –
and it would be all the more
embarrassing for the owner if the dog
had been assisting with a pack of
Foxhounds.

It is a popular misconception that the
Jack Russell Terrier was bred to hunt
rabbit. No such terrier has ever been
bred to pursue a rabbit below ground.
The average wild rabbit will weigh about

one kilogram at the most, so to expect a terrier, weighing at least five times as much, to follow the rabbit below ground is farcical. As well as the obvious difference in size, many rabbit warrens become narrower as the warren progresses further below ground, presenting the terrier with obvious difficulties when trying to return to the surface. It is all too easy for a dog to become trapped by loose soil, resulting in certain death by suffocation if it is not rescued in time.

In this day and age, few Jack Russell Terriers will have the opportunity to assist with a pack of Foxhounds in the pursuit of their quarry. Foxhunting is a minority sport compared to when the Reverend John Russell was alive, and it is not as socially acceptable as it was in the 18th and 19th centuries. However, foxes do continue to cause a problem for farmers, and the terrier is still needed to help with the control of foxes.

HUNTING OTHER QUARRY
Jack Russell Terriers also make excellent ratters, a pastime that many will thoroughly enjoy. When the Jack Russell is at work hunting, whether it is to fox, rat, or a stray housemouse, he has a glow in his eyes and an obvious, undeniable enjoyment of hunting. To see a Jack Russell at work is to see the breed's true character. Do not be tempted to underestimate your Jack Russell's inbred instincts and capabilities. Even the sweetest Russell will normally kill small rodents – and this should be borne in mind in domestic situations if any small mammals, such as hamsters or gerbils, are kept as pets.

In America, where the variety of quarry is more extensive than in Britain, the Jack Russell Terrier is used to hunt a number of animals, ranging from raccoon to groundhog, as well as fox and rat. Competitions are also held in America to test the ability of the Jack Russell as a working terrier.

CHANNELLING THE INSTINCT
Training a Jack Russell to enter to fox is something that requires a certain amount of skill, patience and knowledge. There are fewer professional terriermen around than in previous times, but, if you want to use your terrier for controlling foxes, it is best to enlist the help of someone experienced in the field of work concerned. Many Jack Russells will still retain all the instincts bred for in their ancestors, but these need to be carefully moulded and developed if the terrier is to be spared unnecessary suffering. If a dog is entered to fox with insufficient experience or training, he may sustain unnecessary injuries.

The terrier's instinct to kill small vermin will develop in its own time, usually before the terrier has fully matured. By the age of about ten months, most Jack Russells will be curious about small furry rodents. However, most dogs will not be ready to be entered to fox until they are about eighteen months old, and they should only ever be entered under the supervision of someone with suitable experience. Not all the fox earths that a Russell will encounter will be suitable for entering. The earth may be surrounded by loose soil, or by sand in the case of a coastal fox.

CARING FOR THE WORKING TERRIER
The terrier must be fully vaccinated and up-to-date with his booster vaccinations, since foxes, like other vermin, can harbour a wide range of potentially lethal diseases. Another ailment commonly associated with foxes is mange, which can be passed on to dogs and humans.

The head is the most vulnerable part of the working terrier, and injuries to the

Jack Russell Terriers still retain their hunting instincts, even if they are not worked. No self-respecting Jack Russell can resist the temptation to dig.

To watch a Jack Russell at work is to see his true character.

lips, nose and ears may be sustained. These are all areas where scars resulting from work can be potentially disfiguring. An important point to make is that the majority of the Breed Standards state that scars and injuries resulting from work should not prejudice the terrier's chance in the show ring, unless they interfere with the terrier's movement. However, this stipulation is not included in the interim Breed Standard adopted by the Kennel Club in Britain.

SUMMARY

No matter where you live, and what quarry is applicable in your region, the Jack Russell must be trained for hunting, so enlist the help and advice of someone with suitable experience.

Chapter Five

SHOWING YOUR JACK RUSSELL

When you first take on a Jack Russell puppy, the show ring may seem a rather distant attraction – unless you specifically set out to buy a puppy with show potential. However, many owners become interested in the prospect of showing their dog, and before long, the show-going bug takes over! If you did not specifically choose a 'show' puppy, you may find that the first Jack Russell you compete with may be out-classed. However, you will learn a great deal, and will, hopefully, get a lot of enjoyment from training your dog and taking part in shows. If you decide to get more deeply involved in the show scene, you will be far more knowledgeable when you decide to purchase another dog, and you will already have gained valuable experience in the show ring.

RING TRAINING

If you intend to show your Jack Russell, you must begin training for the show ring as soon as possible. From day one, the terrier should be familiarised with the routine of standing on a table and being examined by a stranger. To begin with, the terrier should only be kept on the table for a few minutes at a time. If the exercise is made too lengthy, the terrier will become bored and will not enjoy the concept of showing. If your Jack Russell Terrier is to become successful in the show ring, it is of the utmost importance that he enjoys being there. Good

conformation and breed type are not enough if the terrier is not happy in the ring and does not show off his attributes.

Ideally, the terrier should have a natural air of self-confidence. The best show dog will be a natural show-off. However, confidence and showmanship should never be confused with aggression. The aggressive terrier will also be on his toes, but he will be eyeing up the competition. For the Jack Russell, this is not typical behaviour and the aggressive Russell, as a direct consequence of his temperament, will not be suitable for the task for which he was originally intended. As such, the terrier is therefore not a good example of the breed, and will be judged as such.

PRESENTATION

Presentation is the all-important word when showing your Jack Russell Terrier, or indeed any breed of dog, and it not only applies to the dog but also to the owner/handler. Although there is no specific dress code for the showing of a dog, inappropriate clothing will draw attention away from the exhibit and towards the exhibitor. The sort of clothing you wear to show your Jack Russell Terrier will depend on the sort of show you have entered. At Hunt Terrier Shows, where the terriers are usually exhibited outside, clothing should be appropriate to reflect the weather conditions – but you should still look

LEFT: If you are serious about exhibiting your Jack Russell Terrier, you should ask the breeder to pick out a puppy with show potential.

BELOW: Show training should start at an early age, keeping the sessions short so that the youngster does not become bored.

ABOVE: Your dog should be presented looking clean and tidy for the judge.

RIGHT: It is the judge's task to assess each dog against the Breed Standard, and then place the entries in order of merit.

smart and tidy. At the major Championship Shows, and in particular when competing with your terrier in the Terrier Group, the owner will need to be a little smarter. Shows such as Crufts, which is attended by many overseas visitors, is definitely an occasion for your 'Sunday best'. Crufts is an indoor show and the vast majority of exhibitors will make more of an effort than would normally be expected for a typical Championship Show. Your exhibit should always be presented clean and tidy, and in good condition both physically and mentally.

THE SHOW SCENE

In Britain, it is only the Parson Jack Russell Terrier that is recognised by the Kennel Club, and, as such, this type alone is eligible for entry at shows under Kennel Club rules and regulations. Many of the dog showing societies will offer classes for the Kennel Club registered Russell. Kennel Club shows range from the Limit show, through the Open show, to the Championship show. Entry fees vary with respect to the type of show and the awards on offer. Obviously, it is best to try entering your dog at a few Limit and Open shows before spending more money on entries for a Championship show. All society schedules show clearly any restrictions on the entering of an exhibit. The rules and regulations for the exhibition of dogs, usually printed with the schedule, should always be studied before entering a show.

As well as the classes available for the registered Russell, there are also many Hunt Terrier shows, which are generally held in the summer months. These offer classes for Jack Russell Terriers, registered or unregistered, and in some cases the classes are split to accommodate the smaller type of terrier also usually referred to as a Jack Russell. Hunt shows commonly offer classes for

Russells of "under twelve inches" and "over twelve inches and up to fifteen inches".

THE JUDGE'S VIEW

The Jack Russell is judged according to the Breed Standard, laid down by the National Kennel Club. The judge must assess each terrier against the Standard, and then place the dogs in order of merit. Why doesn't the same dog win all the time? This is a question that puzzles many novice showgoers. However, the answer is relatively straightforward. Every judge has his or her personal interpretation of the Standard, and so one judge's perception of the 'ideal' Jack Russell may be quite different to someone else's.

The winner should be the dog who looks the best on that particular day, according to the judge's interpretation of the Breed Standard.

INTERPRETATION OF THE PJRT BREED STANDARD

GENERAL APPEARANCE

Built for speed and endurance, the Parson Jack Russell Terrier should appear active and agile. Racy rather than cobby, the length of the body should appear slightly more than the height of the dog at his withers. Ideally, the length of the body from the shoulder blades to the root of the tail should equal the height at the withers, making the length from the point of the forechest to the point of the buttocks greater than the height (at the withers).

CHARACTERISTICS

Essentially a working terrier, the Parson Jack Russell must be of the correct build to enable him to "go to ground" after fox. Correct conformation and temperament are essential in a working terrier, otherwise he will be unfit to perform the task for which he was originally intended.

The Standard asks that the Parson Jack Russell Terrier possess the ability to run with the hounds. In this day and age, few terriers are ever required to "run with hounds". However, the Reverend John Russell made this a requirement of the breed that was to take his name. If the Parson Jack Russell Terrier is to keep its name, it will have to continue to be bred to the Standard as adopted by its creator and cannot be subject to change.

HEAD AND SKULL

The skull of the Parson Jack Russell Terrier should be flat and moderately broad. Very broad heads, such as those seen in the Staffordshire Bull Terrier, are untypical for the Parson Jack Russell Terrier. The same is true of long, weak heads and snipey muzzles, which would put the terrier at a disadvantage should he find himself confronted by a fox. The muzzle should be slightly shorter in length than the length from the stop (point between the eyes) to occiput (point at the back of the skull). The nose should be black with good-sized nostrils. The lips should be thick.

The eyes, which should be dark, almond-shaped and deep-set, should not be set too far apart, nor should they be round or bulbous. Deep-set eyes are less likely to be damaged during the terrier's crusades through the undergrowth in search of viable quarry. Light eyes change the whole expression of the terrier; they look particularly offensive when a Russell has black head markings. The expression of the terrier is very important as this is a major contributory factor to a breed's character and individuality. It is one of the essential elements that contribute to breed "type".

EARS

The ears of the Parson Jack Russell Terrier should be small, V-shaped, and of moderate thickness. They should drop forward with the fold not appearing above the line of the skull. Large, pendulous ears, apart from being untypical, will be more likely to be torn by either fox or rat if the terrier is worked. This also applies to thin ears, regardless of size.

Like the eyes, the shape, size and carriage of the ears contribute greatly to the expression of the dog, and thus, in turn, to breed type. The ears are like a frame for a picture, and correct ear carriage is essential if the terrier is to have the correct expression. Although incorrect ear carriage is unlikely to affect the terrier's suitability for the job he was originally intended to do – providing the ears are of the correct size and thickness – it is a very visual fault and is likely to prejudice the terrier's chances in the show ring.

MOUTH

The jaws of the Jack Russell need to be strong in order that he can defend himself adequately. The bite should be scissor, i.e. where the upper teeth closely overlap the lower. The full dentition of the adult dog should consist of: six incisors, four canines, 16 premolars and 10 molars.

A terrier with an incorrect bite, such as a level (where both the upper teeth and the lower teeth meet), or undershot (where the lower teeth protrude beyond the upper teeth), is more likely to damage and lose his teeth earlier in life than a terrier with the correct bite.

NECK

The Russell neck, when fully extended, should reach beyond the terrier's feet, when lying down or crawling. This will enable the terrier to defend his feet from

Points of the Jack Russell Terrier.

1. Muzzle	*5. Back*	*9. Stifl;e*
2. Stop	*6. Croup*	*10. Tuck up*
3. Occiput	*7. Tail*	*11. Chest*
4. Withers	*8. Hock*	*12. Pastern*

The Jack Russell's head should be moderately broad, with the muzzle being slightly shorter than the length from the stop to the occiput.

Expression is very important in the Jack Russell as this is a major contributory factor to the breed's character and individuality. The eyes should be dark, almond-shaped and deep-set, and not set too far apart.

The head is framed by the small, V-shaped ears which should drop forward. They should not be large, heavy, or pendulous, as they would be vulnerable to injury by either fox or rat if the terrier is working.

a fox when crawling below ground in pursuit of the intended quarry. The muscle in the neck will be somewhat more developed in the stud dog and may form more of an arch.

The neck should not be too long, as this would make the terrier unbalanced. The ability to defend the paws must not be achieved by breeding for shorter legs, as, once again, this would alter the balance of the terrier.

FOREQUARTERS

Correct Russell shoulders should be well-angulated, long and sloping, giving the terrier the freedom and reach of front movement which will enable him to cover the maximum amount of ground with the minimum of effort. Short, upright shoulders result in short steps, using up more energy but covering less ground. When standing, there should be approximately enough room to place three fingers between the front legs of a Jack Russell, at the most four, but certainly no more. At the same time the front legs should not appear as if both legs are coming out of the same hole! Elbows should be straight and perpendicular to the sides. Legs should be straight and of moderate bone. In a terrier with good angulation, the front pasterns will slope slightly.

BODY

The chest at the deepest point, just between the front legs, should not be more than half the height at the withers (the highest point of shoulders). Ideally, the chest should measure about two-fifths of the height at the withers, and should certainly not come down below the dog's elbows.

The Parson Jack Russell Terrier should be spannable, giving an indication of the chest size. The chest is spanned just behind the shoulder blades – and is very important, as a dog that is too deep will

not be able to follow his intended quarry below ground. The circumference of the terrier's chest must be comparable to the chest size of a full-grown vixen fox.

The topline should arch slightly over the loin and flow gently into the tail. The arch created over the loin should be well-muscled, giving greater flexibility. The length of the back should be sufficiently long so that the terrier does not appear square-shaped in profile. There should be a good amount of forechest. Barrel-chested or short-coupled animals are not desirable, and, although they sometimes appear smarter, they are not typical, nor do they have the flexibility of movement that a terrier with the correct ribcage will have.

HINDQUARTERS

Russell hindquarters should be strong and muscular. Both the upper and lower thighs should be strong, with the lower thigh sufficiently long to give a good bend of stifle. Good Russell hocks should be short and straight. The terrier will lack in drive from behind if the hocks are not short. Hocks that are too long may also give the animal a superficial appearance of having a good bend of stifle when this may not be the case. Hocks must be straight when viewed from behind, giving maximum drive.

FEET

The feet of the Russell are important, for they may well have to carry the terrier over many miles of rough ground. Like the hound, thin-soled, open or long-toed feet would not wear well.

TAIL

The Parson Jack Russell Terrier is a breed that is customarily docked. However, with the increasing restrictions on docking, more and more Russells sport the full tail. The English Kennel

Club Standard, as with most of the other Standards for the Jack Russell Terrier, does not yet accommodate the undocked Russell. The Jack Russell Terrier is still a working breed of dog, and docking can be justified in some cases.

The undocked tail should still be of good thickness from the root to the tip, and it will look best if it does not extend below the hock joint. The Jack Russell is not a breed that has been bred with much concern or thought given to the tail length, and subsequently tail length and carriage vary greatly in puppies. Tail carriage in the undocked Russell will often be lower than in a docked specimen and should not be faulted for being so. When working below ground, the tail will be the last part of the terrier to disappear and is regularly used to pull the terrier out from an earth, hence the need for a strong tail that at least provides a good handhold. A terrier that has been docked too short will not have enough of a 'handle' and would therefore be difficult to pull out from an earth or rabbit hole.

GAIT/MOVEMENT
As with the feet of the terrier, the action of the Jack Russell is very important. A terrier with incorrect movement will tire more quickly than one with the characteristic, economical, ground-covering movement, putting him at a disadvantage in the field. Movement should appear effortless and carry the terrier over the maximum amount of ground possible, using the minimum amount of energy to do so. Front and rear movement should always be straight.

COAT
The Russell coat can be either smooth, broken or rough – all are equally typical, providing that the texture and thickness of the coat is correct. In each case, there should be an adequate undercoat which

will be soft and thick, and a straight, harsh top-coat. This will vary in length, depending on the coat type, from approximately 2.5 cms to 5 or 6 cms. The coat should not interfere with the profile of the terrier, and should be short on the legs, head and ears.

The main pattern of growth should be concentrated around the neck and topline, with the characteristic eyebrows and moustache – except in the smooth-coated Russell which will lack these features. The coat should be thick on the stomach and the inside of the legs, offering good protection to the body. The overall texture of the coat should be harsh, but, at the same time, it should be oily and water-repellent, providing good protection from the elements. A healthy coat may, at first touch, feel soft. A harsh texture and a brittle texture should not be confused. A good Jack Russell coat should never feel brittle. A good, thick, loose skin will allow the terrier greater flexibility in restricted environments, such as below ground in the earth of a fox.

MARKINGS
The markings of the Parson Jack Russell Terrier are characteristically confined to the head and root of tail, but, most commonly, they are limited to the head in the traditional badger-marked style, with a white blaze between the eyes. The all-white terrier, and, in particular, the all-white, smooth terrier has to have good conformation and breed characteristics if he is to be a potential show dog, as any fault will be more obvious when there are no pretty patches to mask the faults.

Patches on the body do not affect the terrier's ability to work, and, unless the patches are excessive, the terrier should not be dismissed just because of body colour. But it is important to remember that body colour is not a characteristic of

COAT TEXTURES

The smooth-coated Jack Russell.

The broken-coated Jack Russell

The rough-coated Jack Russell.

MARKINGS

Characteristically, the
Parson Jack Russell has
markings on the head
and the root of the tail,
but most commonly
markings are confined to
the head.

The two different colour patterns both
referred to as tri-colour.

the breed and should not be encouraged in any breeding plan.

Tri-colour markings can appear either as black head and tail markings with tan spots above the eyes and on the sides of the face, under the tail and inside the ears. Or they can be like the traditional hound markings, with the head being coloured tan, and only a small amount of black, if any, between the ears, with any body colour or a tail spot being black or a mixture of black and tan hairs.

Black-and-white dogs, with no tan spots above the eyes or on the cheeks, are not that common, though the amount of tan may vary from virtually none at all to quite prominent spots. The tan colour may vary but should not be red or chestnut colour, while the lemon colouring, though not all that common, may appear as anything from pale lemon through to a pale tan. Some tan-and-white or lemon-and-white terriers may display black around the lips and eyes.

The eye-rims and lips should be pigmented. Even in the all-white terrier, eye-rims and lips should preferably be pigmented.

SIZE
The Standard set by the British Kennel Club for the Parson Jack Russell Terrier sets the ideal height for dogs as 35 cms (14 ins) with a minimum of 33 cms (13 ins); for bitches the ideal is given as 33 cms (13 ins) with a minimum of 30 cms (12 ins). No maximum is set, nor is there any reference to the desired weight of the terrier.

A Parson Jack Russell Terrier that conforms well to the Standard will never appear heavy or cloddy. Bone should be adequately strong, but never so strong as to make the terrier look unbalanced. As a working terrier, spannability is very important in the Parson, and a spannable, well-balanced dog will not usually measure more than 14-14.5 ins.

SUMMARY
Breed type – constituted in the Parson Jack Russell Terrier primarily by correct coat, head, expression, and, above all, temperament – must be of prime consideration in any breeding programme or for any breed judge. It is no good having terriers all of good construction if they lack the essential breed characteristics. It is these individual breed characteristics which make each breed of dog unique.

Good movement should always come with good construction, and this should be given priority over superficial faults such as ear carriage and body colour – neither of which will affect the terrier's ability to perform the task for which he was originally intended.

Chapter Six

BREEDING JACK RUSSELLS

TO BREED OR NOT TO BREED?

The decision to breed from your Jack Russell Terrier is not one that should ever be made lightly, or in haste. Every day an unjustifiable number of perfectly healthy adult dogs and puppies are destroyed because there are simply not enough homes to go round, or because they have been so thoughtlessly bred and are deemed of such an unsuitable disposition that they cannot be re-homed. A litter of puppies will require a great deal of time, not to mention the expense of rearing even a small litter. Can suitable homes be found for *all* the puppies? Is your male Jack Russell Terrier a good enough example of the breed to warrant passing on his characteristics and temperament? An ill-tempered bitch will not be improved as a result of having a litter of puppies. Breeding from such a bitch will only serve to perpetuate the fault.

THE IDEAL MATCH

If you feel justified in your desire to breed a litter of puppies from your bitch, you will need to enlist the help of an experienced dog breeder to help assess the faults of your bitch. It is also important to find someone with knowledge of the relevant pedigrees when searching for a suitable stud dog that will complement your bitch. When assessing any prevalent faults in a line, it is essential to have knowledge of the

pedigree, as the faults may not always be obvious in the individual.

It is important to be honest with yourself when assessing the good and bad points of your bitch. The chosen stud dog must be a good specimen of the breed, he must be free from inherited defects, and he must not double up on any of the faults evident in the bitch. The dog that is likely to sire the best litter of puppies may not necessarily live nearby, and it would be entirely wrong to make geographical convenience a reason for your choice. There are no restrictions on mating individual Jack Russell Terriers with different coat types or with different coloured markings. If your bitch carries some degree of body colouring it will be best if she is mated, not only to a dog that is white or predominantly white, but more importantly to a dog that is known to produce a majority of predominantly white puppies.

GETTING READY

The search for a suitable stud dog will need to begin well in advance of your bitch coming into season, and you will need to book the dog for the time your bitch is likely to be ready for mating. In the time leading up to the beginning of the bitch's oestrus cycle, the owner should ensure that she is not overweight, and that any booster vaccinations are given before the onset of oestrus. The bitch should be in good general health

A bitch that is used for breeding must be a good specimen of the breed, with an impeccable temperament.

The stud dog must complement the bitch, as well as being sound in mind and body.

Mother and son: Breeders strive to produce dogs of similar type that are fine representatives of the breed.

The pregnant bitch should be fed a well-balanced diet and given moderate exercise. She will dictate her own exercise needs as the pregnancy progresses.

and free from parasites such as fleas or worms. Ideally, the bitch should be old enough to have matured both mentally and physically. At the same time, it would be unwise to breed from a maiden bitch that is too old. A good guideline for a first litter is after eighteen months, but certainly before the age of about five years.

THE MATING

As soon as your bitch has shown signs that she has started her season, i.e. the first day that she is seen to be bleeding from her vulva, the owner of the stud dog should be notified and arrangements made for the mating. All bitches vary as to which day is the most ideal for a fertile mating, and so the bitch should be watched carefully for signs that she is willing to accept a mate. The bitch will usually stand with her tail to one side when approached by another dog – and this will usually be around the tenth day following the onset of bleeding. By then the discharge will normally have decreased and become more pink in colour.

It is customary to take the bitch to the stud dog, and then the stud dog owner can assess the suitability of your bitch for mating. If she is not quite ready, then she can be brought back to the dog the following day, or left with the stud dog owner if this is satisfactory to both parties. If your bitch seems totally unwilling to allow herself to be mated, do not attempt to force matters. You can try again when she begins her next cycle, but if she continues to resist the advances of a stud dog, it is better to give up the idea of breeding from her. Most pet bitches that have come from a one-dog family will show some degree of reluctance, which is not really a sign that they do not want to be mated, but is more likely to be the result of a lack in canine socialising at home.

If your bitch is of a good temperament and she is socially well-adjusted, the mating should be quite straightforward. After the dog has mounted the bitch and achieved penetration, the two will remain locked in the characteristic 'tie' for anything from five minutes to one hour or more. No attempt should be made to separate the two during a normal tie. The dog will usually dismount and turn around, and the two will stand back to back. It may be advisable to restrict them at this time by holding on to their collars. The vast majority of matings end in a tie, but it is not essential in order for a mating to be fertile. One mating will probably be quite sufficient to ensure conception, but two matings two days apart is the usual practice and may be preferable. After the bitch has been mated, she will still need to be kept separate from any other male dogs during the rest of her season. Most bitches will still try to escape with any available suitor, and another mating will result in a mixed litter with different sires.

CARE OF THE PREGNANT BITCH

Pregnancy in the dog lasts for an average of sixty-three days (nine weeks). For the first four to five weeks of her pregnancy, the bitch will require little in the way of extra food or special care and attention. However, care does need to be taken that she is not exposed to any infectious diseases or caused any undue stress. The shape of the bitch will be unchanged and, on the whole, her behaviour during this period will remain more or less the same as normal. Some bitches will become somewhat quieter, although in the young maiden bitch there may be little sign of this until the bulk of the growing litter dictates otherwise.

The bitch is a spontaneous ovulator and will ovulate whether she has been mated or not. The release of the ovum (eggs) triggers an increase in the production of the hormone progesterone, an essential contributory factor to the development of the fertilised ovum. However, progesterone is produced whether the bitch has been mated or not as a result of ovulation, and many bitches experience a 'false' pregnancy to some degree. If the mating has been successful, fertilisation of the ovum will occur about seventy-two hours after the mating. The fertilised ovum will not be implanted on the wall of the uterus until approximately 19 days after the mating. This will cause the uterus to begin to swell, although external signs that the uterus has changed shape will not normally be apparent. At around 28 days the developing foetuses can be felt by palpation of the uterus. This should only be done by a vet or other such suitably qualified person. Ultra-sound testing is another method of pregnancy diagnosis and can be performed any time from 28 days after mating.

From about the fifth week of pregnancy there should be a visible increase in the size of the abdomen. This increase will vary depending on the number of developing puppies. At around the same time, the bitch's nipples will begin to increase in size. From now on, the bitch's appetite may begin to increase and she should have her diet adjusted accordingly. However, it is important to remember that the bitch still needs to have her food intake monitored. She should not be allowed to become overweight as this may lead to complications during the whelping. By the sixth week of pregnancy the distension in the abdomen should be quite obvious and the bitch will normally have begun to quieten down, at least a little. The greatest percentage of the puppies' development takes place from about the sixth week onwards, and the distension in the bitch's abdomen will

continue to increase daily. From around the seventh week of pregnancy the foetuses will show up on a radiograph (X-ray). However, the unnecessary exposure of the puppies to such potentially hazardous procedures should be avoided if possible, especially during the earlier stages of pregnancy. This is the only accurate method of determining the exact number of puppies that will be in the litter.

The food intake of the bitch should now have increased by about one third to two-thirds of her normal intake and should be split into two separate meals in the morning and evening. The bitch's diet will also need to be changed to a suitably prepared food for the in-whelp bitch. There are various products available to supplement the bitch's diet, such as calcium compound tablets or specially formulated milk products, specifically for the pregnant and lactating bitch. The instructions for each product need to be carefully followed.

Around the seventh week, the bitch will need to be wormed with a suitable proprietary worming compound. Your veterinary surgeon should be consulted as to the procedure for administering whichever brand of worming product is to be used. There are various products available specially for the puppy and pregnant or lactating bitch in tablet, powder and liquid forms and, providing the directions for use are followed carefully, there will be no ill effect on the bitch or the puppies. The bitch will also need to be wormed following the birth of the puppies and the puppies should be routinely wormed until at least six months of age.

During the eighth and ninth weeks of pregnancy the bitch may rest a lot, especially if she is nurturing a large litter. A whelping box should be provided from about the seventh week of pregnancy onwards. The box should have one side

Whelping is generally a straightforward business for the Jack Russell Terrier. This bitch, Foxwater Frea, has just delivered her first puppy.

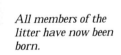

All members of the litter have now been born.

A calm atmosphere will result in a calm mother, who will enjoy the experience of having puppies.

The puppies are born blind – their eyes will open when they are around ten days old

lowered to give the bitch easy access, but it should be high enough to keep in the puppies once they begin crawling. There should be enough room for the bitch to lie down comfortably when fully stretched. Once the box has been provided, the bitch should be encouraged to sleep in it at night. This should help to accustom her to the whelping box in advance of the litter being born, and will make her more likely to settle in it once the puppies have actually arrived. The box needs to be placed somewhere warm and free from draughts. The whelping box, area or kennel will require to be kept at a constant temperature of about 26 degrees Centigrade (80 degrees Fahrenheit). This can be achieved with the use of a heat-lamp suspended above the whelping box, although care will need to be taken to ensure that the bitch does not become overheated.

The floor of the box should be lined with an absorbent material. Newspapers will make perfectly good bedding during the whelping process, but then it is best to use a layer of newspapers covered with a washable, synthetic bedding material.

THE WHELPING

About 24 hours before whelping, the bitch will normally refuse all food and her temperature will drop – a sure sign that whelping is imminent. The normal temperature for a healthy dog is 38.3 – 38.7 degrees C (100.9 -101.7 degrees F), but this will drop by 2 degrees C or so, about 24 hours preceding whelping. The first stages of labour may or may not be apparent. The signs are generally seen as restlessness, leading to the bitch tearing at the newspaper in her bed. This can last from one hour to twelve hours or more. It is a good idea to inform your vet of the date that the bitch is due to whelp and, if possible, to also inform the vet when she has actually started labour.

Do not hesitate to contact your vet should you be at all worried about your bitch's behaviour, for, in the unlikely event of complications, it is important to act as swiftly as possible to ensure the survival of the litter.

Following the first stages of labour, the bitch will begin to start having contractions. As the labour progresses the contractions will become stronger and more frequent. Strong contractions that fail to produce a puppy within about two hours may be sign that something is wrong. Primary uterine inertia is defined as the lack of any contractions and may be the result of obesity, or a dead puppy (in the case of a single puppy). The bitch will usually have started the first stages of labour but fails to progress on to the second stages. Secondary uterine inertia is usually caused by an obstruction in the birth canal, such as a puppy that has become stuck. The bitch will have started contractions normally, and may, or may not, have already produced a puppy or puppies. However, if the continued contractions are non-productive, surgical intervention may be necessary to remove the obstruction.

During the second stages of labour, the bitch will characteristically lie on her side. A series of uterine contractions should produce the puppy, which may be presented either cranially (head-first) or caudally (tail-first), and will usually still be enclosed within the amniotic sac. The sac will either rupture as the puppy makes its entrance or will be ruptured by the bitch. It may be a good idea, especially in the maiden bitch, to ensure that the sac is immediately cleared from the puppy's airways and that the puppy has started breathing. It is important to note whether or not the puppy was delivered with the afterbirth. In the vast majority of cases, this will still be attached via the umbilical cord and will quickly be detached and devoured by the bitch. If the afterbirth has not appeared with the puppy, i.e. if the umbilical cord was broken as the puppy was being delivered, then the bitch should be carefully monitored to ensure that it is passed within a reasonable time following the birth. Retention of the afterbirth will need medical attention to prevent the bitch from becoming ill. However, the retained afterbirth will usually be passed without notice, sometimes within a few hours of the birth. The puppies may arrive at intervals of anything between five minutes and two hours. Providing the bitch is not straining unduly without delivering a puppy, there is no cause for concern. The time of each birth should be noted carefully, along with the birth-weight of the puppy. The birth-weight of the puppy is needed in order that the puppy's development can be properly assessed.

POST-WHELPING CARE
Once all the puppies have arrived, the bitch should settle down with them and begin the job of rearing and caring for her new brood. The maiden bitch may be a little tense and slow to settle after the birth, but if she fails to settle within a few hours of the last puppy being born, this may be an indication that there is something wrong. Once she is quite settled she can be offered a light meal and should certainly have fresh water made available to her. Some bitches will not eat very much for the first day or two after the birth. So long as the bitch seems otherwise healthy, there is nothing to worry about.

Once the litter begins to drain her resources she will not be slow in regaining her appetite (and doubling it!). The use of a proprietary milk supplement for lactating bitches is a good idea at this stage in order to keep the bitch in good condition. By far the biggest drain on the bitch's resources occurs during lactation and her diet needs to reflect this. Once the puppies have arrived, the breeder will then be faced with a dilemma: to dock or not to dock. Under current legislation in Britain the tails of puppies can only be docked by someone who is suitably qualified, i.e. a veterinary surgeon. The tail of the Jack Russell Terrier has for many, many years been customarily docked (although the Parson himself is believed to have left his own terriers undocked), and as such it is not a breed of dog that has been bred with regard to the length, or carriage, of the full tail. If the tails are docked, they should be docked to approximately one-third of the length of the puppy's back. If the tail is docked too short then it will spoil the whole profile of the terrier. Docking should be carried out within the first four days of the birth of the puppies. Dew claws can also be removed at the same time, and this is especially good practice if the puppies have hind dew claws.

For the first three weeks of their lives, the puppies will require little in the way of extra attention from their owner. The bedding should be changed at least once a day and the puppies weighed at regular intervals. At the end of their first week the puppies should have more or less doubled their birth weight. Weaning can begin from about the age of three weeks, starting with milky meals being offered to the puppies. As their demand grows and they become more independent of their mother, the diet can be changed to a suitable complete puppy food. By six weeks of age the puppies should be on about four meals a day. Ask your vet about worming the puppies, as this is essential, and be sure to wash your hands regularly after handling the puppies.

Puppies are best kept with their mother, brothers and sisters until they are at least eight weeks old.

ABOVE: For the first couple of weeks the puppies will divide their time between eating and sleeping.

BELOW: By four weeks of age, the puppies are beginning to explore their surroundings.

Once the puppies are weaned, they become increasingly independent.

At eight weeks of age, this puppy is ready to start life with his new family.

Chapter Seven

HEALTH CARE

The Jack Russell Terrier is a tough little dog, bred to work in demanding conditions. As a result, this is a breed without exaggeration, who will suffer few major health problems. In fact, the Jack Russell is particularly long-lived, and many live beyond fourteen years of age, still enjoying a relatively active life.

Preventative health care is vital in caring for your dog, and it is for this reason that a regular routine of checking your dog is highly recommended (See Chapter Three: Caring for your Jack Russell.) If you know the signs of a healthy dog, you will be quick to notice any abnormalities, such as small lumps or swellings, or any change in behaviour. The owner can become finely attuned to his dog, and spotting trouble at an early stage can be of enormous benefit if treatment is required. A well-balanced diet is also important in keeping your Jack Russell healthy. This should vary depending on your dog's age, and the amount of work he is doing or exercise he is taking. Beware of over-feeding your Jack Russell, as obesity is the prime cause of many health problems. Over-feeding is not a kindness. It can – and frequently does – curtail your dog's life expectancy.

A FIRST-AID KIT
All responsible owners should keep a first-aid kit for those occasions when your dog needs immediate treatment. In most cases, this will be for dealing with minor problems, such as cuts and grazes. In more serious cases, you will need to seek veterinary advice at the first available opportunity.

In the first-aid kit you will need:

A blunt-ended pair of scissors (these will be useful for cutting bandages, etc.)
Cotton-wool
A mild disinfectant
Sterile dressings (these can be purchased individually wrapped)
A roll of surgical tape
Antiseptic wound powder
Antiseptic wound ointment.

Most veterinary practices sell antiseptic products, and will be more than happy to advise on a first-aid kit.

COMMON AILMENTS
During the course of the Jack Russell's life, he may succumb to a variety of common ailments. The majority of these can be treated effectively and without much expense if they are spotted early and the appropriate treatment is administered. In all cases, seek veterinary advice if you are worried about your dog's condition.

ANAL GLANDS
The anal glands may need to be attended to from time to time. These are situated either side of the anal passage. The anal gland has a duct opening into the anal

canal at the anus. The glands secrete a rather foul-smelling substance and may, from time to time, become blocked. The terrier will be seen to be licking at, or trying to lick at, the anal passage. He may drag his back passage along the ground in a bid to relieve the irritation. Occasionally, if unattended, the anal glands may become infected, in which case the dog will require immediate veterinary attention.

The glands can be emptied by applying pressure at either side of the anus. However, it is advisable to leave this to someone with experience – it should not be attempted by the new owner. If the anal glands cause persistent, recurring problems, surgery may help to relieve the dog's suffering.

BITES AND WOUNDS
It is vital that any wound tour jack Russell Terrier sustains receives first-aid as soon as possible. Antiseptic compounds are only effective if used in the first couple of hours. If the wound is particularly deep or is bleeding profusely, it may need stitching and a course of antibiotics from your vet. If the wound becomes red, swollen or inflamed even after first-aid, a course of antibiotics may be required.

COUGHING
Some dogs seem particularly prone to coughs. In most cases, the quicker your dog receives attention, the quicker the recovery will be – and the dog is less likely to develop complications. Veterinary advice should be sought as the coughing may be the result of an obstruction. If the cough is allowed to go untreated, the illness will become more serious, and your dog will most certainly need a course of antibiotics.

DIARRHOEA
If your Jack Russell Terrier has diarrhoea, and no other accompanying symptoms, he should be given no food for 24 hours, allowing access only to fresh water. When you resume feeding, provide chicken or fish for the first couple of meals. However, if the condition is no better or if it worsens at any time, consult your veterinary surgeon.

EAR/EYE INFECTIONS
Infections in the ear or the eye may be caused by a foreign body such as a grass seed. Eye infection can worsen very quickly, so you should seek veterinary advice without delay if you are at all worried. If the eye is runny, it may be that your dog has been sleeping in a draught. Bathe the eye with cotton-wool and warm water, and move the dog's sleeping quarters to a draught-free areas. If the condition does not improve, seek veterinary advice.

HEATSTROKE
Heatstroke may affect the dog at any stage of his life during warm weather. Never leave a dog inside a car in warm weather. Unlike a human, the dog has no ability to sweat through the skin. As the external temperature rises, dogs pant to cool down. In the case of a dog shut inside a car in warm weather, as the external temperature continues to rise, the dog will become increasingly distressed. To begin with the dog will salivate heavily, and will becomes unsteady on his feet. If the temperature continues to rise, the dog will collapse and die.

The heat that builds up inside a car, even in mild weather, can be quite intense and it is best never to shut your Jack Russell Terrier in the car if it is at all warm outside. Kennels and runs should always have adequate shading from strong sunlight.

If your Jack Russell Terrier is found to

be suffering from heatstroke, his body temperature will need to be reduced as quickly as possible. Immersing the dog in cold water, or covering the dog in cold, wet towels is quick and effective. Care must also be taken that the dog's body temperature does not fall too low. As soon as you have administered first-aid treatment, consult your veterinary surgeon as soon as possible.

INSECT STINGS
Bee and wasp stings can have potentially fatal consequences. Bee stings are commonly left in the recipient and, if visible, should be carefully removed. If your dog has been stung in the mouth, it is best to seek veterinary advice without delay. If the tongue begins to swell you will need to ensure that it does not restrict the airways. If you are at all concerned about your dog's behaviour, consult your vet.

PARASITES
ECTOPARASITES
This term applies to those parasites which live outside the dog's body. If left untreated, any ectoparasite may lead to severe irritation, resulting in acute distress and hair loss. If in doubt about any skin condition, consult your veterinary surgeon. A keen eye, accompanying a regular grooming programme, should ensure that any suffering caused by parasitic infestation will be kept to a minimum. An insecticidal spray will give protection against a number of ectoparasites, including fleas, lice, mites and ticks.

FLEAS
Fleas are a common problem in the summer. They can be picked up from a number of hosts – other dogs, cats, hedgehogs and foxes are all possible sources of fleas. Providing the signs for fleas are checked for regularly, the treatment of these irritating little parasites is relatively straightforward.

The terrier's coat should be checked regularly for signs of flea infestation in summer and winter. If you can find fleas in your Jack Russell Terrier's coat, it is likely that it has a great many. Fleas are visible to the naked eye, although they

When you take on a dog, you are responsible for his health care throughout his life.

ABOVE: The Jack Russell is a tough, no-nonsense breed and, with good food and regular exercise, most dogs will lead a long and active life.

RIGHT: Regular grooming will help to keep your Jack Russell free of parasites. It also gives you the opportunity to check for any unusual lumps or bumps. Remember, an early diagnosis often prevents major problems developing.

move through the dog's coat at some speed. Flea 'droppings', which will normally resemble small bits of grit, can be seen, especially near the base of the tail and under the back legs. The flea dirt, when splashed with water, will change to a red colour. The flea droppings are usually accompanied by the onset of intense scratching by the terrier.

If your Jack Russell Terrier is seen to be scratching, he should immediately be checked for signs of fleas. The adult flea will lay up to 200 eggs per day around the dog's living quarters. These will grow into the adult flea after going through a larval stage, feeding on organic matter. The adult flea feeds on the blood of its host and can cause severe irritation. It can also be responsible for the transmission of tapeworm.

If you find signs of fleas, your Jack Russell Terrier will need to be sprayed with a suitable insecticidal spray, as should any other dogs in the house, or any cats, taking care to avoid the eyes and possible inhalation by the dog or the handler. The bedding will also need to be sprayed with a household insecticidal spray, as will any carpets. The initial treatment for fleas should also be accompanied by treatment for tapeworm. During warm weather, it is advisable to adopt a policy of regular preventative treatment for fleas, always taking care to follow the instructions for the use of any insecticide carefully.

HARVEST MITES
Mites can be a common source of irritation in summer. They come from a variety of sources.
The bright red larvae of the harvest mite can be seen in between the dog's toes, and around the eyes and the ears. They feed on lymph and skin tissues causing irritation to the dog. A regular check should be made, particularly if the dog is

seen chewing and licking at his feet. Once again, treatment with a suitable insecticide will be necessary.

LICE
Lice can be seen in the coat as small greyish flakes resembling dandruff. The eggs (nits) are laid directly on the coat, and will appear to be stuck to the hair. Lice can also be responsible for transmitting tapeworm in the dog, and so the initial treatment for lice will need to be accompanied by a treatment for tapeworm.

MANGE
Commonly associated with foxes, most terriers that are used for vermin control are likely to be affected by mange at some time. It is a particularly irritating affliction, caused by mites, and it needs immediate attention. Demodectic and Sarcoptic mange are two forms of common non-host-specific mites. Treatment can be lengthy and should be carried out under veterinary supervision. This could involve antibiotics and the application of medicated washes. Positive diagnosis is made with skin scrapes which are viewed through a microscope. Treatment needs to be thorough if the mite is to be eradicated.

TICKS
Ticks may not be as common as fleas, but they are more likely to cause infection. The adult tick has specially designed mouth parts which enable it to attach itself to the host, where it then feeds on the host's blood. As the tick gorges itself on the blood it will become more evident, and will usually cause the skin around it to become red and swollen. Ticks need to be carefully removed, making sure that the mouth parts are not left embedded in the skin. The best way of doing this is to apply an antiseptic or some insecticidal spray to

the tick. This will cause it to lose its grip on the skin. In some cases, the removal of a tick may need to be accompanied by a course of antibiotics.

ENDOPARASITES
This term applies to parasites that live inside the dog's body. Although there are treatments to eradicate worms, the best course of action is to adopt a routine worming programme, which should keep your dog free of major infestation.

ROUNDWORM
Toxocara Canis (roundworm) is a problem more relevant to the breeding bitch and the puppy under six months old. Toxocara Canis larvae can affect humans and may cause damage to human tissues. Puppies that are infested with roundworms appear pot-bellied, and, if they are carrying a heavy burden of worms, they will also lack condition. Worming with an appropriate compound is essential.

TAPEWORM
The tapeworm *Dipylidium caninum* may affect the adult Jack Russell Terrier throughout his life, and will need regular treatment with a good proprietary worming compound. Tapeworm segments can be seen around the dog's anus, resembling small grains of rice. Fleas carry tapeworms, which infect the dog when the flea is ingested, making worming essential if the dog has been known to harbour fleas. Tapeworms can also affect humans, and a regular routine for worming the adult dog should be adopted by the owner. Make sure that the guidelines for administration of the worming compound are carefully followed.

VOMITING
Vomiting in a dog that generally appears

to be otherwise lively and healthy should be treated with a 24-hour fast to give the stomach a rest. Make sure fresh water is available at all times. If, after 24 hours, the dog continues to vomit, or if the condition worsens at any time during the 24-hour starvation, veterinary attention should be sought without delay.

INHERITED CONDITIONS
There are a vast number of hereditary defects associated with small dogs which may, or may not, be relevant to the Jack Russell Terrier. However, defects do occur from time to time in certain lines, and where this is the case, the breeder of the dog should always be notified. By informing the breeder you will be giving them the chance to take the appropriate action in their breeding plan. It would be unfair to instantly blame the breeder of the dog if a defect has come to light. Defects are usually the result of a combination of recessive genes, and the puppy may have come from two apparently sound and healthy parents, put together in good faith. Such is the nature of dog breeding that unexpected defects will to come to light from time to time.

There are now tests available for most of the hereditary defects, and all Jack Russells used for breeding should be subjected to testing for conditions which are known to occur in the breed. If a breeder continues to breed from a line which is known to produce defects, using affected dogs, the appropriate breed club should be notified. Most breed clubs have a code of ethics to which all its members should adhere.

PERTHES' DISEASE
This is a disease that is not uncommon in small dogs, usually affecting the adolescent. A restriction in the blood supply to the femoral head results in damage to the bone. In mild cases, the

condition will rectify itself. However, in more severe cases, surgical removal of the femoral head may be necessary. The affected dog will usually make a full recovery following surgery. The condition will usually come to light following a knock to the hips, and may or may not be inherited.

PRIMARY LENS LUXATION

A condition seen commonly in terriers. The supporting ligament of the lens may break as a result of trauma, but will more frequently be the result of an inherited defect. In most cases the condition will lead to blindness.

HEREDITARY CATARACT

Cataracts will cause the eye to become cloudy and commonly result in blindness. The cataracts can in certain cases be operated on but with limited success.

LUXATING PATELLAS

Essentially a slipping kneecap, the condition will vary in severity, and affects the movement of the dog which will be seen to 'skip' when walking. It is almost always an inherited condition, and affected animals should not be bred from.

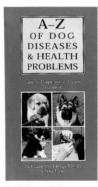
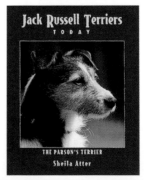
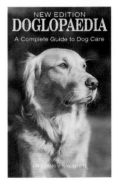